SHORT CUTS

INTRODUCTIONS TO FILM STUDIES

FILM THEORY

CREATING A CINEMATIC GRAMMAR

FELICITY COLMAN

WALLFLOWER

LONDON and NEW YORK

A Wallflower Press Book

Wallflower Press is an imprint of
Columbia University Press
Publishers Since 1893
New York . Chichester, West Sussex
cup.columbia.edu

A complete CIP record is available from the Library of Congress

ISBN 978-0-231-16973-8 (pbk. : alk. paper)
ISBN 978-0-231-85060-5 (e-book)

Columbia University Press books are printed on permanent and durable acid-free paper.
This book is printed on paper with recycled content.

Printed in the United States of America

p 10 9 8 7 6 5 4 3 2 1

CONTENTS

ACKNOWLEDGEMENTS

Thank you to the students and teachers of film theory that I have worked with, and all encounters that have helped my thinking on and through this discipline, especially Angela Ndalianis and Barbara Creed.

Special thanks to Apollonia Zikos, Erin Stapleton, Anna Hickey-Moody, Roy and Dr Tang, who have helped me immeasurably in vital moments.

Thanks to Yoram Allon, Commissioning Editor at Wallflower Press, for his tireless support of the discipline of film studies.

INTRODUCTION: THE WRITTEN MATTER OF
A CINEMATIC GRAMMAR

Writing about Werner Herzog's documentary film *Grizzly Man* (2005) in *Cineaste* magazine, Conrad Geller reminds his readers of one of the unforgettable scenes of the bear-loving naturalist, Timothy Treadwell. Geller writes of a moment selected by Herzog from Treadwell's video blog, where Timothy is 'fondling a large pile of bear dung. It was, he says, produced by one of his familiar bears, Wendy. "It's still warm" he says wonderingly. "It was inside of her!"' Geller characterises this film through such scenes, later asking 'Did Treadwell do some good?' He concludes that *Grizzly Man* 'comes down to a kind of metaphysical debate between Treadwell and Herzog' (2005: 52–3).

The type of approach that Geller takes typifies contemporary writing about film. An affectively resonant scene from a film is re-drawn with words with emotive emphasis (*fondling; wonderingly*), a conceptual index is applied to the film (*metaphysical*), and a philosophical argument concerning *ethics* is drawn in with the question of 'doing good'. But how would we describe Geller's own mode of theorisation? Would we label him a Marxist theorist as he looks to the relationship between Treadwell's social world of film production and that world's continuation of social inequities and hierarchies (not the least between man and animal)? Or would we categorise him using a phenomenological approach, where the 'encounter' is deliberately not reduced to representational terms, but can only be personified in terms of its sensate dimensions (for example, see Sobchack 2004)? Geller further asks us to consider *auteurist* theory (see Bazin 2008), with his equalising reference for both director and film subject (such as we see in other theoretical accounts of Herzog, such as Noys 2007). Or should we set up a polemic with Geller, and state that in fact what he describes is not metaphysical, but more to the point, a *post*-metaphysical, realist narrative (such as Ruiz 1995 might suggest), that is, contingent upon his authorial position as a spectator of the spectacle of 'beast, man, and nature'? In fact, all of these approximations might be considered, but there are yet numerous other approaches we could take to analysing this curious film.

What is film theory?
Film theory is a written interaction *with* and *of* the images and objects and ideas produced *in* and *of* film, and the cinema industry. The film theorist is a transdisciplinary practitioner, a writer of sound-images, connecting the temporally determining worlds of moving sound-images with the material-ity of writing. The work of these practitioners, as I explore in this book, creates and utilises a filmic grammar, one specific to the expression of the cinematographic. This grammar ranges from the opinionated story about watching a film of choice, to the construction of a rigorous technical theoretical system of analysis, to the production of speculative thought, abstract ideas that may or may not be realised. The theory may be class, race or gender specific, or it may be couched in broader terms, where 'everyone' is a complicit viewer. The grammar can be enriched through intergenerational, transdisciplinary and transtechnological research and teaching. Or the grammar shows itself to be gender-blind, racially imper-vious, politically, philosophically and theologically biased, and can be patronisingly colonial and/or patriarchal in tone.

In the first two decades of the twenty-first century, film theory is still marked by its medium obsession – *look what this new technology can do!; and look, here is another site of a demolished movie theatre*. But, as much as it must adhere to the restraints of a discipline that went under the university's official radar for quite a while, being taught in classes such as Anthropology, Art History, Enthnography, English, Gender, Languages, Music, Sociology, Philosophy, film theory has been largely sidelined by the perceived vocational popularity of Media Studies in universities, and its fate is ironically somewhat more secure than other humanities disciplines, many of which from that list have been subject to cuts in the early twenty-first century (such as Gender Studies departments). It arrives, and is funded there, along with broadcast media, animation and games studies, as a technological medium that is recognised as playing a central role in politics and culture, and which can reap huge political and economic benefits.[1] Meanwhile, as a commercial industry, filmmaking has shown itself to be forever tied to national funding models, restrictions of censorship and political ideological impositions, as the subject of propagandist themes, and the peddler of militarism, sexism, homophobia, racism and a general xenophobia. Regulation of the commercial markets in filmmaking (and I am not talking of the porn industry here) do provide some protections necessary for actions against women, and children, and some film theories will either list, or name some arenas of abuse on screen (cf. Projansky 2001; Wheatley 2009: 134; Hines and Kerr 2012). As an artistic practice, filmmaking is less constrained by the ties of the commercial market's regulation by government and national censorship and regulatory bodies, and more self-regulated by funding opportunities, access to resources and opportunities for development. All types of filmmaking production are subject to the global as well as local economic and technological fluctuations, and both of these factors have determined many different outcomes for the practice and reception of filmmaking (see discussions on this by Elcott 2011: 45; Stiegler 2011: 35ff).

The core theoretical concepts of twentieth-century film thinking – auteur theory, psychoanalytic analysis, cognitive analysis, apparatus theory, feminist critique, post-colonial deconstruction – are still used and are useful. In 1987 Dana Polan called for film theory to be 're-assessed', stating: 'I will want to argue that, to be most useful, Film Theory should cease to exist as such' (1987: n.p.). Polan's comments are from the end of a decade of significant change in film theorisation, and they signal an historical time where a paradigmatic shift in the discipline occurred. Polan was right – the medium and the economics of distribution and the marketplaces have changed, as have consumer desires, and those disciplinary staples have been replenished and augmented in terms of their discussion of what film is and how it works. For example, in the time-span of the late 1980s to the 2010s, commercial screen-based technologies shifted from recording using analog to digital technologies. In the coming decades, further informational and technological changes are anticipated with the augmentation of digital with bio-platforms, and the continual modification and use of analog and digital for aesthetic and economic reasons.

It produces more images, more worlds, more objects and ideas to comprehend and write about. Unlike Polan's call, this book will not be critiquing what film theory *is* and what its utility might or could be.[2] Rather, this book aims to offer overviews of existing film theorisation, focusing on specific examples, and signal ways that this body of work enables different models of thinking about film that point to some of the future possibilities of and for film theory. What is at stake in our current moment as the poststructuralist theoretical legacy encounters new thinking concerning gender, feminism, decolonisation, political economy, materialism, embodiment, information networks, art, technology, performance, data storage, archives and digital platforms is another significant turning point for the practice of film theory. Film itself, as a technological medium, is undergoing significant changes in terms of the ways in which it is produced. Although it is a child of the twentieth century, it has in many eyes been outperformed by its younger, more agile siblings – television, gaming screens and mobile media – and military and government uses of film techniques, where surveillance, satellite and GPS screens dominate the perceptual field once the sole domain of the movies.

Aims of this book

This book has two inter-related aims, each of these are addressed to the student and the teacher of film, practitioner and theorist alike.

The first aim is to provide an accessible framework for thinking about the diverse practices and breadth of film theory. There are many very good books that outline core themes for film theory that detail the existing arguments, theoretical positions and their methods for analysis and exegesis (cf. Fischer 1989; Rony 1996; Guneratne and Dissanayake 2003; Galt 2006; Lapsley and Westlake 2006; Rushton and Bettinson 2010; Furstenau 2010). This book is an introduction to thinking about film theory; however, it invites the reader to turn those defined concepts into questions, and form new research agendas – ones that are of relevance to the reader, and their worlds, and to thinking about issues exterior to the reader's life that films expose them to.

The second aim is to connect the practices with the key historical points in the discipline. This book will quickly sketch out the core theoretical-historical premises and practices that provide the academic frameworks that one has to necessarily work with and against when engaging in a certain discipline's activities. This is important as the invention of new paradigms of thinking and different neologisms draws many criticisms that reject the cyclical terms of fashion.[3] Film theorists apply terms that draw from and/or reject historical and contextual thinking. Theoretical methodologies applied to film theorisation in the 2010s such as posthumanism, accelerationism, object-oriented ontologies, digital technologies and new materialism may retrospectively be the 'postmodernisms' of the 1980s, but how they play out is yet to happen. And this is the thing that film theory does: imagine, describe, hypothesise; not necessarily in that order, or all at the same time, but in putting forward positions and theorisations, there is evidenced in the words and texts of theory a scale of sharing of knowledge and ideas. A generosity of thinking can slide to an absolute pronouncement. There are the material facts of a film's production and chemical and digital composition, and there are empirical, cognitive, speculative and connected theories. This book seeks to sketch out some different paradigms for thinking about what film theory is, how it works and what it produces by revisiting some of the core historical approaches to film theorisation while re-defining frames of reference. For students of film theory, this can be a gradual process. Film theorisation also involves a different technique of writing than that of film criticism (which tends to be a responsive and descriptive, rather than analytic, practice), and philosophy of film (which is more speculative, and seeks to create rather than describe), although there are many cross-overs with both forms of writing.[4]

The question of what film theorisation is for is addressed throughout. In answering the question, *What is cinema?* posed by André Bazin, we can first respond simply, and modify as we qualify the enquiry (see Andrew 2010). Cinema is a technological medium that captures moving images and sound and through its mechanisms it creates images and movements that change over time. Interfaces with the film object and experience of film vary through technological changes, consumer design and artistic practices, but the viewer or spectator of and in film is always implicated as a participant. As visual practices change, so too does language mutate to articulate and express the senses of change in perceptual practices due in part to technologies (cf. Crary 1990; Jay 1994; Parks 2005; Shaviro 2010), and through political changes that affect the construction and production of different types of images (cf. Ravetto 2001; Rancière 2004; Beller 2006;

Jin 2006; Rancière 2009; Halberstam 2011; Pick 2011; MacCormack 2012; Beller 2013; Colebrook 2014). As paradigms of vision affecting epistemological material, histories and interfaces change significantly over time, so too does theory modify and mutate into something else. Theoretical histories and critical analyses no longer just point to technical changes in filmmaking as an industrial medium, or aesthetic changes in filmmaking as a creative art form, the ideological and biopolitical changes (where the classification and hierarchisation of cultural bodies change over time), but also attend to the geopolitical changes in the world, which impact upon the flows of information and resourcing of the film industry.

This volume is an exploration of the theories created or used by film theorists. The writing of film theory is in itself a creative practice. It is a writing that provides a theory of another creative practice. Yet filmmaking engages a medium arguably far more complex than the medium of writing. Writing is undertaken in response to and provoked by a range of interlocutors, writes itself as a response to sensorial, affective, instrumental, technological, historical stimulation. It may be a poetic act or it may be instrumental, it may take a polemical tone, an accusatory, a hagiographic tone, it may be precise and analytic in expression, or it may be full of baroque grammatical and rhetorical flourish and laboured expression. It produces concepts, arguments and histories. It may stimulate critical or reactionary thought, it may produce something new, or refresh something in the mind of the reader/receiver of the theory; however, it may be judged to be 'good or bad' theory. In its broadest sense then, film theory is an object unto itself; sometimes fully immersed in its object of reference (film, the cinema, the film image, the cinematic sound), but also operating at the other end of that scale where a singular film is not the primary focus of the theory. Both positions and all that fall in between this spectrum are productive of this object of study; what is film theory?

Film theory is a practice that uses the medium of language to write (and to speak) in response to a different medium altogether, one that creates visual and auditory moving images by using very specific technologies. Within the field of Media Studies, film is its own discreet object, no less subject to the terms of its own lived mediation of its 'active' and 'ethical' practice of 'transforming matter' (see Kember and Zylinska 2012: xvi-xvii; 71). Film produces its own film language; as many cinematographers, scriptwriters, directors and producers of film attest, there is a creative, and ethical (meaning to decide on a certain action and form), imperative that theorists describe in terms of its cinematic grammar, and detail in specific cases. This book takes the position that film theory is a form of writing that produces a unique cinematic grammar, which is in turn mediated by its readers and users.

Here I engage the word 'grammar' to infer a number of possible meanings and contexts. In addition to the filmic grammar of the tools of filmmaking is the linguistic meaning of grammar. As with other forms of writing, film theory attends to the arrangement of words, to direct and to redirect their lexical meaning, enabling a play of words, just as an edited play of images on screen can redirect the contextual meanings of discreet objects. In addition to these two standard uses of grammar and film theoretical writing, I extend the term grammar through Bernard Stiegler's concept of 'grammatisation'. Stiegler renegotiates aspects of Derrida's 'grammatology' (a thesis concerned with the de-centering of structures [see Derrida 1976; Gaston and Maclachlan 2011]). Where Derrida's grammatology was intented to overthrow the speech-writing hierarchy, Stiegler's grammatisation repositions technological culture as the writing of the world. Grammatisation is an open-ended term that articulates how societies hold and develop the literal tools of 'culture', which are reliant upon memory, itself subjected to and mediated by industrialisation processes (see Stiegler 2010, 2012). Memory requires 'prosthetics', Stiegler argues (2011: 60). These prosthetics include recording technologies such as books, records, photographs and film, necessary for cultural memories to be maintained and be reproducible. Stiegler's theory describes how societies have different technological systems and models with which to remember their cultural practices. This memory takes three different stages; first, the primary experiences of passing time, second are secondary retentions of the memory of those passages, and third are the tertiary forms of retention of experience and memory, through externalised processes. Grammatisation thus describes the techniques and systems with which a society will maintain and feed its externalisation of memory models. Stiegler's grammatisation is a concept that is not without its critics (cf. Lebedeva 2009; Bunyard 2012) and discussants (cf. Hansen 2004; Barker 2009; Kember and Zylinska 2012: 167), as it tends to draw a universalist paradigm of the affects that capitalist visual cultures have had over its consumers. Thus Stiegler's polemic glosses over those consumers in terms of their different genders, ethnicities, class experiences of those cultural forms. In this book, I apply grammatisation as a positive term and as a way of indicating and connecting certain points where a convergence of technological epistemes of film occurs in theorisation. Similar to how Foucault's archaeologies of the controls of subjectivity and sexuality (1978; 2008), or Haraway's account of gender and technology (1991) provide modes of historicisation, grammatisation engenders discussion of the conceptualisation of material conditions – which need to be situated (in terms of their human, political and geographic factors) before being specific.

Thinking about film theory: methodological approaches
The vocabulary of film theory as applied often reads as inadequate to the experience of the film event. When film theory draws up its model to express what it sees or experiences 'at the movies' then a mismatch or disjunction from what other theories describe can occur. Film theory invents new expressions to accommodate and capture and express the film event. But the questions of whose event?, facilitated through which modes of technological access (privileged by race, class or gender?) and from what position (what systems are in play?, what agential concepts?) is it viewed (spectatorial intent?) remain politically problematic but are nonetheless vital questions for the theorist to ask herself. There are many different ways of doing film theory, the polemics of which are not the concern of this book (for some of the conflicting positions on the practice of film theory see Carroll 1988b; Smith 2010; Sinnerbrink 2010, 2011: 13ff; Clayton and Klevan 2012; Buckland 2012b).

This book approaches film theory in an empirical sense, by highlighting some core connections that cinematic grammars have created. This is done so with the intention to share conceptions as well as raise issues and ideas, with the aim that theoretical consideration can facilitate all kinds of relationships of the present and future writing of the making and the realised cinematic. It is not the intention of this book to proclaim either the 'truth' or 'falsity' of theories, or the accuracy of any of the grammars invented or used. That is for the reader to test. As the theoretical work done attests, cinematic grammatisation can facilitate all manner of connections. It remains up to the user how to apply them, and to decide for what purpose.

In using the multiple aspects of the term grammar, this volume takes the grammar of the film theorist to explore the common questions of the discipline. This approach is in itself a question that film theorists' pose, one that they critique in the prose of others, and a historical point in film theoretical work that offers ways of 'reading', 'hearing' and 'seeing' film as a cinematic language. It should be noted that this book sets out with the intention not to advocate one way or another as the 'right' or 'wrong' way to do film theory. Some theories focus upon the visuals and not the sound, some do both, some do cognitive, some do sociological readings, and so on.

Like all grammars, film theory forms part of the system of rules that govern a language, and is thus applicable to a wider range of media forms. In their creation, film theories contribute an epistemological resource that connects the technologies of filmmaking and film composition. This book explores these connections through film theorisation of processes of the modeling of cinematic matters (territory, temporality, politics, subjectivity) of the filmic world into specific discourses of film. Film theory uses a specific critical discourse, what this book describes as a cinematic grammar of creation. The grammar of this theory, the matter of its creation, and the forms of its address in relation to the film world – ideas, concepts, other theories, technics, and spectators – are discussed in the following chapters.

Film theory is a particular mode of writing that we can identify through the form and places of its practice. The film theorist is the *explicador* of the film, writing not only of the film object, but also of the film experience and its position within contemporaneous critical discourses with their political and thus aesthetic limiting factors. While philosophies of film are primarily concerned with the ontological implications of film-as-object, film theory has always had a broader remit. Film theory writes about the technical aspects of film (the script, production, industry constraints, national markets, festivals, censorship, institutions, marketing, screening, distribution, preservation) and the critical discourses that the film event creates. Both aspects contribute to the knowledge economy of the film; its epistemology. In writing the grammar of this epistemology of creation, film theory not only performs the activity of recording its contemporaneous event, but also enters the film event and film technology into an active dialogue and performative connection with other film events and technologies.

Describing a methodology that is applied, or used, or developed in a film theory can involve a very technical form of writing. A methodology applied, however, is different from a method taken. So when writing a response to a film, or to a question concerning film theory, one might begin by thinking about what method to take: (i) What aspect of the film or theory is of interest? (ii) What is the political agenda, or agential issue held in mind when using the film images to write? (iii) What is it about the film/image/theory/sound that has inspired the thinking or writing about or responding to this work? Answers to each of these questions will use a different method to then create their own writing form. The first response may involve an analytical method that turns then to cognitive or feminist methodologies and methodological tools in order to respond. The answer to the second question may develop through individuated (culturally given, intuited or experiential) knowledge. The third question requires rephrasing after consideration of the first two. The question would be: how does the film/image/theory/sound make one think, and act? Some film theory texts provide now historicised names for this 'how' question, detailing methods that in fact are the agents for thinking: formalism, modernism, narratology, psychoanalysis, phenomenology, postmodernism, realism, structuralism, and so on. Other film theories focus on the how question, by examining the structures and modes of individuated agency, through terms such as affect, agency, cognitive analyses, deconstruction, ethics, schizoanalysis, semiotic studies, and so on.

As with any theoretical approach, methodologies are beset with limitations for thinking and application. Common problems encountered with film theory include:

- limitations of a concept application
- too broad a proposal
- categorical errors of argument
- ahistorical comparisons where the temporal context of the viewer and of the subject are collapsed
- comparative arguments: compare *to* means liken to; compare *with* means make a comparison
- inadequately evidenced arguments, such as reception theories.
- how does the author know (God-like) what an audience/viewer experiences in front of a singular or series of films?
- racial bias
- ethnic bias

- gender biases in play in the analysis
- epistemic focus that ignores technological determinates
- exclusion of political context

Paradigms of film theory: models, technology, spectators
In this book, I divide the polyphonic grammars of film theory by reference paradigms; points with which theory navigates its personal aesthetic and produces and demonstrates a specific theoretical position, whether explicitly stated or not. First, I consider the ways in which film theory diagrammatises its filmic objects and creates film theoretical concepts that have a very specific purpose by modeling. Second, I look at the types of film theoretical positions on technology, an often neglected aspect of film theory. Third, I consider the ways in which film theories engaging the subject of spectator/s, and the subject of film, have produced a thus far fairly anthropocentric cluster of thoughts, expressions, associations, modifications and new theoretical conversations that themselves are a part of the production of film work.

Feeding into and within each of these three reference points – models, technology, spectators (the titles of the three chapters of this book) – are the main ways that film theory organises its object; as a technologically conceived and produced object, and as an account or event. In each approach, film theory is writing an epistemic grammar of the cinematic, each with a specific intention to situate the film as something. Under these terms we might ask what separates the theorist of film from the philosopher of film? While the philosopher of film might answer that they are in pursuit of what might be the ontological thing of the film, the film theorist might provide a more representative answer, in accounting for the contextual and industrial form that the film has been able to assume. It is difficult to generalise, and impossible to account for all the forms and regional variations of filmmaking practice, so it is intended that the following discussion provides a framework for thinking about the aspects of film in which the reader is interested, without being prescriptive or dismissive of existing scholarship.

Chapter 1: Models
I use the term 'model' to infer that the model is distinct from the film, or film sound-image that produced it, and it does not always directly refer to

that image in a direct way. A 'model' also infers some kind of pre-determination, such as we have to work with in academic disciplines, where a 'normative' standard operates. Film theory as practiced and taught will thus first refer to its normative model before it might innovate, or investigate, the possibility of creating something new, or of opening a different pathway for thinking, and thus theorising. This form of theory – normative standard and difference (most obvious in Hollywood v. Art Cinema comparisons) – has the effect of creating a dialectical structure, where the binary of same/different makes it impossible to detail differences with any innovative thinking. The style of writing within the discipline has changed over its one hundred-plus years of work, as writing styles and language usage change according to the technologies facilitating expression. In film theory these changes in style are seen, for example, in the early 2000s with the advent of blogging techniques, and open-access academic publishing, where journals such as *Senses of Cinema*, or *Rouge* provide refereed, academic open-access film theory (as opposed to the pay-per-institution, or individual access of commercial publishers, where authors must pay to access their own – unpaid – work) and with the increase in more fictionalised narratives of theory (which always existed, but were not accepted as potential canonic texts; see for example, Pasolini 2005). The terms of film theory are not the absolute blueprints for designing a model (despite the insistence on 'canonic' texts), but do function to provide paradigms, boundaries and invitations for theorisation. However, it can be fatiguing for the student and teacher to approach writing about film through the textual diet of the standard classificatory models of film theory when looking for ways to articulate a film experience, technique, interest, concept or history, however commercial, avant-garde, challenging or confirmative that film may be.

Because there are so many different types of models that film theory utilises, I have chosen to focus on two complementary areas of theory that problematise the notions of film theory's grammatical practices of modeling: the semiotic and the material. In this choice I display my own methodological bias, by drawing on the work done on Félix Guattari's diagrammatic approach to his philosophical/psychiatric practice, as mapped out by Gary Genosko (2009) and Janell Watson (2009).

Chapter 2: Technology
This chapter explores the different ways that technology, and the technology image, can be theorised. Technologies direct our thinking of the aestheticisation, commodification and mediation of all ideas and activities. The consideration of the technological and the technology of film underpins theoretical models of films. Often, a focus on the technology of the film is couched in quite different ways to a film theory that is concerned to describe or narrativise film. Film is an industrial technology and as industry, its material is subject to the laws of the market in which it is created, produced, distributed and consumed. Film theory is not always attentive in making connections between the technology of filmmaking and its forms. Discussion of the practical or the material processes of this industrial medium has been somewhat limited to focus upon specific arenas, such as to film sound theory (cf. Brophy 1998, 1999, 2002; Chion 2005, 2009; Harper *et al.* 2006; Altman 2007), or to the formal innovations of technology (in a modernist sense), but has also expanded the language of film theory through making new connections and implications of different technology and its politics (cf. De Lauretis 1987; Bolter and Grusin 2000; Hubbs 2004; Beller 2006; Keeling 2007; Shaviro 2010; Halberstam 2011). In particular, new forms of use of cheaper, more flexible technologies for filming and flexible computer coding and input programming devices (such as Arduino, Raspberry Pi, Makey Makey) enable new kinds of film processes to be made. The technological platform used will always affect the content, but what are the questions for film theory when discussing technology? Using the conceptual framework of three different films – *Pine Barrens* (Nancy Holt, 1975), *Daughters of the Dust* (Julie Dash, 1991) and *Cosmopolis* (David Cronenberg, 2012), the chapter explores the notion of technology-images, and indicates how different theoretical positions on this topic (for example, Doane 2002; Virilio 2005; Stiegler 2011) have redirected the spine of what film theory is and can be.

Chapter 3: Spectators
In this chapter I explore aspects of the subject, subjectivity and spectatorship in order to observe the differences and similarities, and overlaps in their use, as users, in film theory. Instead of looking at where film theory has defined spectatorship in terms of a predicative role – that is, for example, the spectator as fan, as horror genre lover, as feminist,

I examine some of the roles that film theory has assigned the spectator, who, for example, may be a user of 'Netflix grammar' (see Madrigal 2014), or who may be seeking some form of 'identification' with the performers on screen (see Mulvey 1986). Film theory can be descriptive as well as analytic, and a question to ask of the theory is in terms of its scope – is it framing an issue of instrumentality? – leading to the design of the spectator by the film and its analysis of the terms and visual logics that films produce. Transdisciplinary work across gender and feminist issues concerning technological cultures (cf. Haraway 1991; Butler 1993; Hayles 2005; Halberstam 2011: 78ff), in physics (Barad 2007), science and technology have fuelled a new materialist critique that examines the informational codes that create meanings (Haraway 1991: 161ff) and the political ecology of things (Alaimo and Hekman 2008; Bennett 2010; Coole and Frost 2010). The terms of current theoretical debates for film theory are still writing with the 1960/1970s materialist and structuralist film debates, film and cultural studies, gender, political, economic and geological work engaged and debating the material production of the film, inclusive of the economic, ecological and political terms of the complex spectator, her environment and the ethics of her construction. After post-structuralist critiques, the posthuman and the non-human figure more prominently across film theory.

Writing film theory

Film theory sometimes promises a universal analysis of a film, yet in doing so it displays its discursively limited constitution. In film theoretical analysis we find the instrumental and the poetic modes of reception and response to a film work. There can be a focus on the possible ideas generated and harvested by the cinema, yet analysis of these ideas is contingent upon the political and aesthetic position of the author/s of the film theory. It is a recognisably distinctive mode of writing, yet film theory shares commonalities with other writing modes that are responsive to the cinema, such as film criticism and philosophies of film. There is no singularly identified 'correct' film theoretical position. The commonality to be found in film theory is its medium, that is, its use of language as spoken and as written text in order to describe, interpret, analyse or read the medium of film, where film is a moving sound image, and or the cinema as an industry is also variously addressed as a text, or work.

As a discipline, the range of approaches to film theory's subjects, in terms of methods, aims and philosophical positions, are readily identifiable through practices that signal their acceptance of certain theoretical legacies and hierarchies of the particular methodological, and thus political, position and potential agency. By this we might take any film, for example, where the ethics of its world as presented could be either celebrated or afford a reflective critical disagreement. Or we might take a film whose 'meaning' is contestable. Film theories should be able to tackle any of those positions and provide some analysis of the operation of the image, plus its significance.

The field can be broadly divided between those film theories practicing an applied or technical (practical) exposition, and those film theories engaged in work aimed at critically creating new schematic or innovative theorisation. Sometimes the discipline is divided by analytic vs. continental methodologies, but there is too much crossover of research aims and intentions to see that as an absolute categorical divider. Within these divisions are many sub-categories for theorisation, which can also be classified by their methods and aims, and how far they might stray from their orthodox positions. Each and every position taken has a specific political and aesthetic legacy behind it, where even the nonsensical or abstract position holds just as much 'meaning' and political resonance as a theory that declares itself to be concerned with sensibility or concrete issues. This volume is not concerned with definitions of the 'meanings' of the content of films or the cinema, but implicitly does concern itself with how those things are prescribed and created by and in film theories. This book identifies some of the core theoretical positions and their critical contributions to the discipline of film theory, but it can only indicate some of the areas that film theory investigates. The few filmic examples I use are for signposting ideas for the reader; readers should be able to substitute a film that they are thinking about to test their own modeling. In this book I focus on the film theoretical aspect of the discipline. The philosophy of film, or film-philosophy, engages another discipline, that of the writing of philosophy, which some will see as just another theoretical position, while others regard it as distinctive. Where crossovers are produced I signal them, but a comparative discussion of film theory and film philosophy is not the focus of this book. This book does not attempt to be an exhaustive survey text, rather it presents theories for their indicative work, or influence in the discipline. There are many voices absent here, this does not indicate that I thought they were not of value, but for the sake of economy and polemical narrative, there is necessarily some editing for economy. I would also note that while I display certain biases toward theoretical positions, this book is not intended to provide a standpoint on one or another theoretical model. Rather, this book seeks to offer ways in which the reader might think about the connective points for theorising screen-based media such as film. Multiple examples are given so that the reader can find an access point to the discussion. Connective points are made through concepts that shift over time, such as the terms of spectatorship, the notion of a cinematic landscape or territory, considerations of temporality, politics, ethics, subjectivity, or the consideration of materiality and technology. As connectives, their grammar, and the terms of their grammatisation, provide commentary on what is unique about film theory as an interdisciplinary study of visual cultures; a technologically materialist theory of audio visual media forms.

The writing of film theory involves the invention of different types and styles of inscriptive systems. The grammatical practice of film theory is something often commented upon, as writing is the medium. Amongst theorists, there are many variations of opinion on the topic (see, for example, Metz 1974a, 1974b; Heath and Mellencamp 1983). Noël Carroll states, unequivocally: 'Cinema is not a language' (1996: 187), but immediately has to qualify this absolute. He argues a case for the term 'verbal image' ('primed', or 'proper') for media forms, including filmmaking, that allude to the visual, even though their medium may be neither word nor image. There are many kinds of languages – visual, verbal, auditory, sensory; language is a slippery term, and in this sense suitably ambiguous for writing about a medium such as film, which similarly has no definitive 'purpose' or 'meaning', but film has and is put to absolute purpose, that of ideological media supports for various political propaganda.

The grammar of film theory is like any language; in order to use and engage it, one has to learn the rules thoroughly, before being able to be able to break them. But in having to learn the rules, much of what is practiced under film theory can be dull, predictable and uncritical of itself. There are standard terms that one expects to find in a discussion labeled film theory, yet after over a hundred years of film theory practice, this grammar is showing signs not of a 'crisis' but instead the opposite, of a renewal into something different; the creation of new rules by new users who are not limited by the canonic texts or historical rules of authorship and critical practices. But it is also the result of a development of the film industry, where a genuine passion and enthusiasm for the medium and discussion of all aspects of the medium has proliferated the language. The encouragement of transdisciplinary work in education and research practices has also resulted in some fertile connections between ideas and knowledge. Those rules have been broken; in many places their historical systems remain but the potential for different, perhaps more robust, ways of being in dialogue with the film and the film industry are appearing. The grammar of film is expanding. While some theorists may say that this expansion is due to the expansion of the film industry and its products, not all theorists would agree. Changes are due to a myriad of reasons: the politics of each territory; the changes in educational equity; the ongoing activities of militarism in different regions of the globe; the unstable and iniquitous economic systems in action around the globe; the changes in technologies such as digital media forms; the changes in the film industries' capacity for distribution and reception; the changes in educational discipline specificity; the film product is in most cases a collaborative effort, which involves modification, testing and development of ideas before completion.

Film theory is not about studying or applying some form of blanket dogma, as Pauline Kael (1966), Bill Nichols (1991), Raúl Ruiz (1995) and Christine Gledhill and Linda Williams (2000) (among others) remind us. Theory provides us with tools for thinking, a method with which to approach a film, and a conceptual structure to hang onto when meaning starts to slip away. Theory enables us to deconstruct representations, and grasp issues larger than ourselves through access to other dimensions, as produced in a filmic world. Contemporary cinema has changed and contemporary theory has moved to accommodate shifts in theorising the nature of contemporary film, and the development of a cinematic consciousness of the differences of activity and of imagination within the world. The following chapters explore film theories' concepts in terms of how they present connections of ideas as economies of knowledge for film analysis.

Notes
1   See Polan 2007 for an account of film 'instruction' in the US; De Brigard 1975 on the use of film in ethnography; Elsaesser and Hagener 2010 on

the changing structures of film theory study.

2   For books that explain what film theory is and its utility, from a range of modeling viewpoints, see Diawara 1993; Young 1995; Dyer 2001; Codell 2006; Rushton and Bettison 2010; Andrew 2010; Etherington-Wright and Doughty 2011; Thornham 2012; Andrews 2013.

3   See Barthes (1990a) and Baudrillard (1996) for discussion on fashion cycles.

4   For examples of cross-over writing that uses both disciplinary methods of film theory and philosophy of film, see Bellour 2000; Buckland 2000b; Bolton 2011.

1   MODELS

je
tu
il   elle

– opening title-frame, *Je, tu, il, elle* (Chantal Akerman, 1974)

Film theory books are full of models. Their contents pages list the methods, systems and the schemata with which one might analyse a film, a
film sound-image and/or the cinema industry. In writing empirical nota-
tions on the production, construction and then summary and analysis of
the choice and cinematography involved in the images, materials (audio
and visual), the use or rejection of a specific theoretical model determines
ways of thinking about the film. In this modeling, a measurement system
is enacted. Measurements imply values. Whose values are they? They
change across historical and cultural contexts. The type of theoretical
model used determines the structural agency of the theory, as applied. The
systems of analysis that film theories create describe the light and sound
waves, chemical and/or digital and/or biological data that comprise an
image, its site of reception, the technologies and materials that it uses,

and then model that image into a system of expression. What is important, significant or publishable, is contingent upon standards set from within the system. To change a standard model requires an intervention into language and conceptualisation. Often film theories themselves will have a self-reflexive aim or, as with philosophy of film, construct their entire work around a type of model they employ for their intentions for theorisation. D. N. Rodowick has noted that 'a discipline's coherence derives not from the objects it examines, but rather from the concepts and methods it mobilizes to generate critical thought' (2007: viii).

In this chapter I use the terms 'model' and 'modeling' to indicate that there is a design of theory being articulated by a film theory; its concepts and methods. Film theories seek to define a film, an idea that the film has generated, a sound; in essence, the image expressed, holistically. How does theory define this image; give a definition of the film? Firstly, it produces an analysis of the film image by either working with the film's mode of production, or producing a system of thinking that sits alongside the audiovisual work. In the literary, written and diagrammatised terms of film theory, this can initially require separation of the information from the content, and observation of the thematic and structural elements by which the larger information of the film is housed (genre, form, style, main players, production details), from the actual film event itself. Consideration is taken for intentionality – is this a parody or serious in context? The ontological nature of film (a philosophical question that I skim over in this text) is such that it produces sound-images that were not at all expected, planned or the point of the film is to generate the unknown, or chance, or the often utopically framed quest for 'the new'. Secondly, as the truism states – any tale involves a teller – so the first question of film theory is: what is the aesthetic – and thus political – mode of the 'teller' of the tale of the image? That is, by what modeling of a situation or condition or character do we come to know the tale? These questions apply to all forms of film: non-narrative, abstract, art, documentary, narrative, animated, 3D, analog, digital. The film already has been modeled, perhaps by the script, the sound design, an actor's performance, or a director.

The practice of film theory is like other humanities-related disciplines in that 'rules' and standards exist for discussion within an intelligible model, in order to produce a system of analysis, or non-system. This model in turn provides structural shape and sound for the subject matter of the spectator who is held up as the identity test for the theory – in terms of her body, class, race, gender, ability, historicity of her media and so on, within a specific context. Implicitly then, this measurement or rejection of the standard engages a judgement, whether in pronunciation of a different way or by building upon the work already done. Models contain their own aesthetics and ethics (by historical allusions, no matter the film form, for example, whether in first-generation structuralist filmmaking, or in Hollywood musicals), and sometimes one reads in film theory a certain moralism that comes in defining the syntax and rules of the system of theory in engagement. In other words, the choice of model is a discussion that involves an aesthetic account of a film based on what I like and what you do not like, sometimes with reasons provided. The question of which theory with which to model an argument, or craft an analysis of film, often becomes the subject matter of the theory, and this is a problem for film theory that I take up in the following chapter on technology.

Figuring the model and its method is not just a matter of having film theoretical literacy. It also involves consideration of the contextual senses of the work, looking for the components of the argument that might be fruitfully brokered into creating diverse connections. If we pause to observe two approaches to film theory modeling, we can begin to explore some grammatical schema in play.

First, a book on film theory itself: Dudley Andrew's *The Major Film Theories* (1976). Andrew notes in his preface that his book aims to 'set off the major theorists one against the other, forcing them to speak to common issues, making them reveal the basis of their thought' (1976: v). He uses a simple three-part schema with which to model that common language: (i) 'The Formative Tradition' (including sections on Munsterberg, Arnheim, Eisenstein, Balázs); (ii) 'Realist Film Theory' (Kracauer and Bazin); and (iii) 'Contemporary French Film Theory' (Mitry, Metz, Ayfre and Agel). Drawing on a common Western film language, Andrew includes references to a few films from the classic European and Hollywood canons and discusses specific scenes where theorists address these films, noting their language and approach, using these to build his own theory concerning the 'correct' way to read the film, and comment on different filmmakers' own processes of filmmaking. Within his tripartite model, Andrew further organises his arguments concerning techniques, such as 'form and function', the difference between 'naturalised' and 'defamilialisation' (in both theory and practice) (1976: 80–4), 'mechanistic' [meaning structuralist at that time] versus 'organic' theory and practice, creative properties and phenomenology. He makes some very specific comments concerning 'truth', for example in discussion of Sergei Eisenstein's film theory and filmmaking practice he writes: 'Even Eisenstein recognized the inadequacy and immorality of willful montage creation which tries to manipulate the spectator' (1976: 67). The films addressed by Andrew include *Umberto D* (Vittorio De Sica, 1952), *La Terra Trema* (Luchino Visconti 1948), *Diary of a Country Priest* (Robert Bresson, 1951), *Strike* (Sergei Eisenstein, 1925), *The Treasure of Sierre Madre* (John Huston, 1948), *Citizen Kane* (Orson Welles, 1941) and *Nanook of the North* (Robert Flaherty, 1922). A review of the book in *Jump Cut* outlines the pitfalls of Andrew's model for film theory, including a critique of the all-male line up of theorists, the exclusion of the avant-garde voice by the focus on mainstream cinema, and a lack of relevance for those interested in 'politically engaged film theory' (Jenkins 1978). Andrew's text is indicative of the mode of narrative-based textual theory that set the scene for the end of the twentieth century. His subsequent film theorisation includes a self-critique (familiar to any instructor who has had to deliver all-encompassing, and thus distancing, film survey classes), where he points to the disciplinary state of world cinema studies that discourages the broad survey in favour of attentive singular complexity. Here his modeling tool is cartographic, a 'mapping' that he defines by its interests in the political, the demographic, the linguistic, orientation, and topographical mapping (see Andrew 2006).

My second example of the modeling structures that a book of film theory designs is one that offers a model based on the industry of cinema itself, through the carbon footprint upon the terrestrial worlds it inhabits and by which it is produced. Nadia Bozak's *The Cinematic Footprint: Lights, Camera, Natural Resources* (2012) offers a grammatisation of the hydrocarbon economy that is required to support the film industry. Bozak critiques the theorisation of authors such as D. N. Rodowick and W. J. Mitchell, who describe the sculpting and recording of light by the film process, countering with a reminder of the matter of the universe: 'Before the sun makes the world visible, it makes it possible' (2012: 19). Bozak's model employs the language of sustainability – with chapters titled 'energy', 'resource', 'extraction', 'excess' and 'waste' – pointing out that the cinema industry and filmmaking, in both analog and digital forms, is a product of and contributor to Earth's finite resources. Like Andrew, the film examples that Bozak draws upon are recognisable and accessible for most Western audiences: *An Inconvenient Truth* (Al Gore, 2006); *Blackboards* (Samira Makhmalbaf, 2000); *Empire* (Andy Warhol, 1964), but unlike Andrew, Bozak crafts new readings of these films according to her thesis of the cinema as a carbon-based producer and consumer. In Bozak's thesis, the long-screening, energy-sucking film *Empire* is thus modeled as a consumerist critique of 'excess'. Stephen Rust, Salma Monani and Sean Cubitt (2012) have described Bozak's thesis as part of 'Fourth Cinema'; cinema that is concerned with 'cultural and environmental concerns' of cinema production. This form of modeling casts Bozak's theory as 'Other' (see Bhabha 1983), in terms of national film markets, so the address of whether the cinema should be regarded as 'not just industrialised but [a] "hydrocarbonized" system' (Bozak 2012: 4) is never taken up. Modeled as Fourth Cinema means that content (and meaning) is predicated by a structural hierarchisation of what it is not: it is not First Cinema (the mainstream international film market, dominated by Hollywood); Second Cinema (art-house film); Third Cinema (indigenous issues). (For the extensive discussions on the economic, industrial and numerical modeling of different cinemas see, for example, Gabriel 1982; Chanan 1983; Downing 1986; Armes 1987; Solanas and Gettino 2000; Guneratne and Dissanayake 2003; Shohat and Stam 2003; Leotta 2011: 108.)

There are many other examples I could have begun with; the filmmaker artist's monograph, or an anthology of writing on film by filmmaker-theorists; a book on a specific auteur, or one on a regional cinema. Film theory models are varied, but their contextual production can make connections that accord an aesthetic and political value to the work – of writing, and of film production. Film theory has joined with many other disciplines to model and write concepts for thinking about film, including art history and practice, gender and cultural studies, education, philosophy, sociology.[1] As a dynamic technology, film cultures produce and maintain the agential mechanisms for embedding or disembedding information. This is the semiotic and material agency that film theories seek to articulate through recognisable discourse.

Agency is modified by qualifiers concerned with specifically produced bodies (of culture, politics, social institutions and standards), and filmmaking orients itself around the telling of stories using a range of tools from textual analysis (such as genre, or critical, queer, Feminist, race, post-colonial theories [cf. Young 1995; Aaron 2004; Codell 2006]), so as to narrate the identity, gender, sexuality, racial profile and migratory politics of those bodies, and/or referencing itself as a material agency, directed by its technological platform, or medium. From the study of film theories, I regard this as a spatialised process of media grammatisation, where the agential platform (the medium of film, or other media screens, written texts) is not only involved in a degree of recording, but in a process of reordering and auditing (as in sound audit) of the physical and imagined worlds. Thus, for example, a film, and the theorisation of a film on the narrative of an indigenous revolt against colonisation processes of indigenous territories, conveys (semiotic) information about the story but also (with varying degrees) conveys (material) information about the [technical] process of telling the [biopolitical] story (see for example, *Rabbit-Proof Fence*, Philip Noyce, 2002; Collins and Davis 2004: 133ff). What that looks, sounds and reads like is contingent on a range of additional agential factors, including production funding, and artistic aesthetic and political orientation.

To describe this media grammatisation, and its qualifying agents, I consider the core areas of modeling theories that have emerged from film theory; the semiotic and the material. Within these two areas lie the variations and nuances of the practice of the model. Theory tends to engage its broad stroke summation by its chosen method of modeling, and declare its interest by the qualification, or schematisation, of that use. For the economy of this chapter, I explore just some aspects of these modeling forms.

First, I explore the semiotic analyses, under which I include theories of sound, psychoanalytic, post/modernist, post/structuralist, cognitive forms, phenomenology, schizoanalytic, affect. Second are the materialist analyses, which include auteurist, feminist, post-colonial, national cinemas, ecological, temporal, spatial and structuralist film theories. This topography of the dominant approaches is not an exhaustive account of the different types of theory that are used in film analysis, and I group theoretical methodologies here by their textual modalities. Through this mapping, different connective possibilities can be drawn. These approaches are not exclusive, and often a theory will draw from different forms of analysis and produce a hybrid system, often connecting methods from different approaches, sometimes adopting a purely formal method.

The modeling requires a subject in addition to the topics and forms of film, and these are the topics of the following two chapters, on technology and on the spectator. In approaching semiotics of cinema and including under this umbrella the diverse methods and practices of theorisation, I want to point to some commonalities for the sake of clarity in this diverse and ever expanding field, and suggest some revision of old and invention of new ways of designing film theory. First, I will sketch out some of the main debates in this arena.

Modeled meanings

Cinesemiology, historical structuralist theory and *cinécriture* such as those written by Christian Metz, Peter Wollen and Agnès Varda's respective propositions (amongst others), arose from the historical juncture of a post-avant-garde era of filmmaking. While Metz was in pursuit of a practical system, Wollen saught to account for the materiality of culture and Varda was in pursuit of the vernacular truth. In a way these three very different approaches are the reactive foils against models of theorisation that aimed to provide a more systemic, 'scientific' account of the images that film, and the cinema, produce. Different levels of rejection of any poetic, or surrealist, positions are evident in the tone and language of theories using the methods of structural and, later, cognitive semiology. Cognitive models are the 'how it works' of film theory (see, for example, Bordwell and Thompson 2012). I call it the *cabin in the woods* approach: you have a limited set of resources and you must economically apply them to fit numerous purposes. Outlining the tools to be applied, explanations are provided for any kind of inchoate image that film may produce. The constructed image is deconstructed, by taking apart its various component parts with its self-defined tools, which often appeal to the reader's common sense, but where any superfluous details are ignored, or rejected by theory (see Eleftheriotis 2010: 45).

Common threads of the cognitive model include a concern with the interpretation and analysis of 'film language'; the 'syntax' of the film image as recognised, and used as a technique by Russian Formalists (see Stam *et al.* 1992: 28). Editing techniques, as in the work of Sergei Eisenstein and Dziga Vertov, are thought of as the film's semiotic system, where image and sound editing is used to affect a manipulation of the recorded images which, once positioned in, can produce a particular sequence that will have certain affective outcomes for the overall film, and for the narrative. Both Eisenstein and Vertov published positioning manifesto film theories; Eisenstein's arguably having the most impact on contemporary film theory with his essay 'Montage of Attractions' (later taken up by Tom Gunning, 1986), where he argues for a montage of 'aggressive moments'. Eisenstein's editing techniques were thought to be so affective in terms of their revolutionary potential that he was made by the Stalinist State to cease his revolutionary-semiotic production and produce non-ideologically deconstructive/provocative images.[2] David Bordwell, who put aside Eisenstein's Leninist desires to pursue the construction of the film form, applies the cognitive formal rules that the Russian filmmakers investigated, producing a particular vein of cognitive semiotic modeling that has been very popular for teaching a pragmatic cinema history (see Bordwell 1985; Bordwell and Thompson 2012).

Interested in the potential revolutionary device of semiotic analysis, feminist film theory of the late 1970s onwards joined elements of structuralist semiotic analysis with the psychoanalytic theories of Lacan, Freud and Klein, to develop post-structuralist, sometimes post-anthropocentric semiotics (cf. Creed 1993; Modleski 2005) that was heavily criticised for its attempt at a grand all-encompassing theory (despite the criticism coming from those who were arguing for their own standpoint position but seemed unaware of their own ideological structures). In their 1996 book, titled *Post-Theory: Reconstructing Film Studies*, David Bordwell and Noël Carroll argue against the use of the application of psychoanalytic theory to film, in particular they unleash a scathing attack on theories including Marxism, Post/Structuralism and Lacanian psychoanalysis, instead promoting a film theory model of empirical cognition, based on their spectatorial cognitive-as-normative model and non-cognitive as deviation. This binarist exclusive position provoked a flurry of responses to *Post-Theory* and a sharp division between theoretical practices (see Grønstad 2002 for a discussion of the issues; also Buckland 2012a: 114; Cubitt's lament against cognitive modeling, 2004: 4; Harbord's proposal for a different approach, 2007; Elsaesser and Hagener's spatialisation of film studies, 2010). If Bordwell and Carroll's subtitle of 'reconstructing' is set as oppositional to the feminist mandate to 'deconstruct' (which we discuss in chapter three here), then the other thing that a purely semiotic-cognitive analysis does not allow for is an account of the poetic, chance and the personal. However, critical models of all kinds often begin with an anecdotal account, and turn that experiential response to a filmic world into a theoretical point, which acts as a connective for an applied reading of a specific model.

While it is a common enough analysis in contemporary film theory to use the terms of acousmatic, affect, allusion, apparatus, binarism, classic, code, diegetic, diegesis, discourse, icon, ideology, index, intertext, inter-, multi- or trans-textual, message, non-diegetic, meme, narrative, panoptic, paratext, realism, representation, rhetoric, sign, signification, semantic, symbol, scopic, text and textual, unit and voyeuristic, this vocabulary was only established in the last quarter of the twentieth-century of film theoretical practice (and still debated in terms of application, meaning and utility). These terms all grew out of the need to articulate the nature of film as a constructed and heavily coded medium – whether the theory was arguing for film as an art form, or as a commercial vehicle, or as the creation of a new reality. Francesco Casetti provides a partial overview of the main players in these theories (1999: 132ff), and Robert Stam, Robert Burgoyne and Sandy Flitterman-Lewis (1992) give definitions of terms; however, this is still an arena of film theory that has only a partial historical account. Because different signs have different cultural, and thus political, contextual meanings, the application of semiotic analysis to film theory opened multiple ways for thinking about analysis itself. As a structuralist tool, formal semiotic analysis looks purely at the coding given by particular signs in a text, does not separate the cultural meanings from the given signs, and examines how the overall text functions within its system. Hong Zeng has argued that the study of film semiotics 'has not done enough to probe specific cultural motifs' (2012: 160). However, the semiology of world cinemas attends to this perceived disparity (cf. Downing 1986; Armes 1987; Chaudhuri 2005; Codell 2006; Martin-Jones 2011).

Although dominated by the Eurocentric male viewpoint, many minority and non-Western voices are represented in the film theoretical histories that currently come under the discipline's specific descriptions of 'national' and 'world' cinemas, and the numerical First to Fourth Cinemas. Through such modeling, these theories signal (in the semiotic sense of sign, symbol, icon, meaning) as Lùcia Nagib has pointed out, a certain imbalanced hierarchical structure that infers a mostly mythical 'centre' against which they are measured (2006: 30). Counter to the attractive, utopic, but most often theoretically unaccountable ideas of a grand or all-encompassing theory, specific semiotic histories of cinemas and film communities are written. The rubric of 'world' cinemas defines specific semiotic-communities, that actually always existed, but which film theory has been a little slow to publish. The critique against semiotic-community theory is that is can be too closed, too parochial, and too political. We see this in all kinds of theoretical positions, from the avant-garde, experimental artist communities of different regions and eras, to discussions of commercial cinemas.

Semiotic modeling
Semiotic modeling in film theory has produced, and continues to produce, a vast range of positions, and subjects. Semiotic modeling can be used as a political tool that theory engages, or as a form of cultural logic that enables film analysis. By including within semiotic modeling the theorisation of not just structuralist avant-garde works (from where the terminology and ideas originated), but also qualifiers of world, transient, deviant, amateur, transnational, experimental, feminist, queer, postcolonial, and so on, and using modeling tools including affective, cognitive, narrative, psychoanalytic and phenomenological methodologies, where the theorisation leads to in terms of the logic of its argument, is entirely contingent upon its model's structure.

What the model usually does is provide a unit for its value orientation. If you imagine the family unit, in all of its variables, as a value-orienting unit, then the notion of theoretical modeling unfolds. Pier Paolo Pasolini's *Theorem* (*Teorema,* 1968) may help this dry theoretical necessity (like the family unit) be a little more palatable, so I write the following with this film as the orienting unit for thinking through theories of semiotic modeling. Pasolini viewed the middle-class family to be completely contemptuous, and like 'the idea of the Nation, the idea of God, the idea of the confessional Church' to be completely 'on the wrong track' (Pasolini [1968 interview], cited in Stack 1969: 157). Although he had written the film treatment for *Theorem* years before, Pasolini says it took him a long time before he could bring himself to film it; to be able to depict the 'vulgarity' of the bourgeoise, and the lack of ability of either 'dissident bourgeoise' or 'natural bourgeoise' to solve the problems presented by the petit bourgeoise (Pasolini in Stack 1969: 157–8). *Theorem* begins with every conservative politician's nightmare: the collapse of capitalism with events not limited to abstract numbers on a computer screen, but tangible, physical acts of collapsing the capitalist walls where they are strongest – in the world of managerial hierarchies, and within the home, the places that produce and maintain the body of the worker. Images of a media scrum outside a factory reveal that the owner of the factor, a managerial professional whose salary is statistically likely to be more than two hundred times more than any of his workers, has given his profit-making venture over to those that actually run it and produce the profit. The camera pans slowly across the bleak scene, a model factory, with hangers for all kinds of machines. When and why did this system ever become so desirable? Aren't there always more workers than managers? Why don't workers revolt sooner? In Pasolini's script, in return for the dissolution of the hierarchy of the factory, the manager's family is blessed with a visit from an angel of inauguration (Terence Stamp, wearing fawn-coloured polyester slacks), who assists in facilitating a new family model, whose value-orientation for society is unclear.

Film theory semiotics draws its terminology from a number of distinctive forms of linguistic semiology.[3] There are many variations within the family of signs. When reading film theory, it is worth checking against the two ends of the family, comparing Pasolini's post-Kantian approach to sound and image, and his concept of 'free indirect discourse/relationship' (as Deleuze adopts it, 1989: 261), with Metz's discourse of the image (or variations of), which seeks very specific definitions for images.

The main theorists (outside of film theory) include Charles Sanders Peirce, Ferdinand de Saussure and Louis Hjelmslev. For the sake of economy, I shall just look at the first two here. C. S. Peirce's system is indexically based, where anything can be a sign. Peircian terminology pervades the grammar of film theory, in particular through the work of Gilles Deleuze (1986, 1989), and Deleuzian film theory that draws from the Peircian semiotic language (although not always its original meaning). In a massive text, Johannes Ehrat wades through Peircian semiotics to model theories of narrativity, but does not provide any system for application of his analysis (2004: 247), an approach not unlike the continuum of signs in *Theorem*. Like Deleuze, Richard Dyer draws upon Peirce for his terminology, rather than the content (as Ehrat does), to assist him in in describing the 'affective codes' of musicals (2002: 20). Peirce uses a tripartite typology to describe signs: first, the categorisation of signs, as phenomenological categories of qualisign, first, second and third; second, as topological categories of icon, image, symbol; and third, as rhemes [terms], dicisign [propositions] and argument. Peirce describes how the sign is an image which stands for another image (its object), through the relation of a third image (interpretant), this in turn being a sign, and so on (see Deledalle 2000). For example, in a Peircian reading, the appearance of the Visitor (Stamp) in *Theorem* is an image that is an indexical sign of change. In more pragmatic filmmaking, the colour red is an image that is often used as an indexical sign of love or hatred (for example, see *Zentropa* [Lars von Trier, 1991]).

De Saussure's work has been more widely adopted in film theory as a linguistic semiotic system.[4] Criticism of De Saussurean semiotics will point to how it draws from pre-existing structures (ie, the rules that enable organisation) which do not enable or allow free thinking or creativity but which limit thinking to the structures we already access and use. In other words, an individual is constructed by the language that they have access to, a feminist deconstructive critique which Teresa De Lauretis points out in the opening story about Alice in *Alice Doesn't: Feminism, Semiotics, Cinema* (1984). Quoting from Bakhtin, De Lauretis notes that language is 'over-populated – with the intentions of others'; in the looking-glass world that Alice inhabits is 'the world of discourse and of asymmetry, whose arbitrary rules work to displace the subject, Alice, from any possibility of naturalistic identification' (1984: 1). De Saussure called the basic elements of language signs, where in language we can agree that a word is something that is arbitrary and substitutable, within the rules of grammatical context. In writing the family unit, Pasolini grammatises its image into the over-populated landscape that De Lauretis defined. Terence Stamp's character interacts with the family of the ex-factory owner, a Milanese bourgeois family. He is a visitor, yet is also the host, a catalyst, a crack, a provocation to become-other. He is more Peircian than De Sausurrean. His presence saturates the family unit with affective possibilities; after making love to each of the family in turn – the Maid, the Daughter, the Son, the Mother, the Father (and perhaps even the family Dog), they all experience separate revelations or epiphanies and they subsequently feel the need to confess and either withdraw, meditate or talk about this experience with him. Through their contact with this god of capital, all the characters in *Theorem* suffer various types of nervous breakdowns and breakthroughs, and completely alter their lives – they stop talking, they levitate, become suicidal, become genius – they have reached, as Deleuze describes a schizophrenic state, a 'breaking through and a collapse' (quoted in Guattari 2008: 65); and an 'erasure' of subjectivity ensues (Tong 2001: 88). We see most characters become 'useless' in terms of their economic subjectivity, which relies upon a certain degree of ability to engage and communicate within their unit and within their gender-appropriate societal-roles. The family unit is completely dissolved.

De Lauretis's point is to turn the structuralist rules of semiotic analysis into subversive semiotic discourse about gender role limitations, as played out in cultural texts. Her film theoretical modeling applies these principles of feminist semiotics on other film theoretical texts, one example being a reading against Stephen Heath's reading of Nagisa Ôshima's *In the Realm of the Senses* (*Ai no korîda,* 1976) (see De Lauretis 1984: 28ff).[5] The variance in Heath and De Lauretis's argument comes down to a dis-agreement about the theoretical reading of the film text's 'positioning' of the spectator; where one theory posits the spectator as a semiotic index of gender (De Lauretis), and the other the spectator as a component of the perceptual machine [as a technology], one that performs a semiotically coded, psychologically-driven labour role in order to complete the film (Heath 1981). What both semiotically-driven positions are dialectically revelatory of is gender difference (rather than diversity), and the ideological forms of politics they ascribe to Ôshima's film. My own Guattarian semiotic reading of both theoretical positions would point to the 'semiotic micro-politics' at work under both types of modeling schemes, where the subject as defined by Heath and De Lauretis can only ever oscillate between the two positions (see Guattari 2013: 181; for a discussion of Guattari's position on cinema see Genosko 2009). My point being that there are many different ways that a semiotics of interpretation is used in film theory. Pasolini said that Stamp's character in *Theorem* is either the Devil or God (cited in Stack 1969: 157), but I see him as a thief of energy; he is pure capital: absolute, desirable and completely abstract.

Semiotic registers can be bound in their determination of a binarist either/or modeling system (analytic/poetic; normative/alternative; old/new, and so on), but they *could* also articulate post-structural models for thinking through film, as I describe below with materialist models of film theory. First, let us take a minor detour around the Second Generation Semioticians (if the first are Kracauer, Vertov, Eisenstein).

Christian Metz, Pier Paolo Pasolini, Umberto Eco and Peter Wollen are the polarising theorists written into histories of film semiotics. Each deserves more attention than space permits me here. I focus this discussion around Metz (with Pasolini hovering). His key work, *Film Language: A Semiotics of the Cinema* (1974a), includes his essay from 1964, 'Le cinéma: langue ou langage?' Metz's *langue* (language system) comes from De Saussure's language circuit of substitution. Metz's discourse of the image seeks very specific definitions for images.

Metz proposed a cinesemiotics that rejects the notion that film is structured like a language, but that it does in fact have its own language, which theory should read as a system of signs. Metz's *grand syntagmatique* theory developed in the early 1970s, and argues (after De Saussure) that film is a discourse because it organises itself into recognisable narrative forms that are productive of signifying procedures (see Stam *et al.* 1992: 37). Francesco Casetti debates the details of Metz's *langue* or *langage* (language) and comments that his work exemplifies a 'style' of film 'methodology' that is 'based on the rejection of essentialism and on the adherence to method' (1999: 133ff). Taking umbrage with Metz's positing of cinesemiotics as the 'Great Men Theory of Cinema', Constance Penley criticises Metz for his lack of citation of his disciplinary field and the work already done on semiology by 'his predecessors like Bazin, Astruc and Pasolini' (1975a). Despite Penley's caution, Metz's work continues to appear as the point of authoritative evidence for film theoretical arguments.

Authority is relative. In the manner of Vittorio De Sica's soothsayer in *The Bicycle Thieves* (*Ladri di biciclette*, 1948) (the woman with a crystal ball who can see all over the city of Rome), Pasolini delivers a commentary of the use-value of the Catholic Church when the maid of *Theorem* becomes a saint and ultimately sacrifices her body to the continuing 'mythos' of Italian construction, literally laying her body into the foundational earth at one of the massive postwar public housing projects in Roma (see Nerenberg 2006: 177). In this way, Pasolini shows how even in the absence of the familial unit and its attendant labour requirements, other pre-existing institutions exist as barriers to any new constitution of subjectivity outside of the socialised worker-body. While the workers' bodies are released from enslavement, pre-constituted social, medical, theological, artistic constitutions of the individual within capitalism are sustained. Thus, says Pasolini, *Theorem*'s end remains 'suspended' (Pasolini in Stack

1969: 157), in the dialectical impasse that politics of the twentieth century found itself located.

Materialist models

Metz's *Film Language* was translated from French into English in 1974 and its reception revealed the different pathways and interests that film theory was taking in specific communities at that time. In addressing the terms and defining the significance of Metz for film theoretical analysis, Warren Buckland provides the institutional context for semiotics adaption by the discipline (2012a: 74–7), marking a shift in modeling by enabling what is essentially a political commentary on the discipline's terms of configuration (see also Buckland 2000b and 2004 on film semiotics). The implications of *Film Language* are still being played out, as a turn to a semiotics of 'reality' (cf. Zizek 1992; Rushton 2011), or a turn to a post-linguistic materialism. Also described as 'new feminist materialism', Iris Van der Tuin defines as three pathways for this re-turn to materialist modeling. She notes that this movement investigates (i) 'the posthumanist theorization of agential matter'; (ii) 'the theoretical impetus of biopolitics and bioethics ("political matters")'; and (iii) a 'non-linear take on political economy (2011: 6).

The contemporary interest in the posthuman and the non-human model resonates with the post-media theorisation of the mediation of technology (see Hayles 1999; Winthrop-Young *et al.* 2013); and theoretical work on world cinemas, post-colonial, decolonial, queer and feminist film investigates the second and third area that Van der Tuin identifies (cf. hooks 1996; Rony 1996; Projansky 2001; Aaron 2004; Williams 2008). For film theory's specific discipline, the historical materialist models of first generation (Kracauer) and second generation (Metz, Gidal, Varda) are only now productive of third generation materialist film theories (Beller, Cubitt, Stiegler), with the digital platform providing a different conceptualisation as well as practice (which I discuss in the next chapter).

Early twentieth-century film theorists had already proposed the examination of the correlation between language and the facilitation of the material film image.[6] Later theorists and filmmakers extended the speculation to include the practical language of filmmaking, and the articulation of the materiality of its sound and image (cf. Burch 1973: 90). Throughout Pasolini's *Theorem*, parts of Mozart's famous 'Requiem Mass for the Dead' is used as extra-diegetic music. The section *Introitus Requiem Aeternam* ('grant them eternal rest'), accompanies multiple scenes throughout the film, acting as a sound sign that curves, as it (indirectly) introduces various scenes of Pasolini's allegory of death of the middle classes. Pasolini achieves an extended image in *Theorem* through a number of means, through the use of the requiem, by producing a film that has very little dialogue (only 923 spoken words), by engaging as many 'long takes' of extended scenes (without intercutting) as possible, using acting styles that are muted, and with minimal expressions (see Pasolini in Stack 1969: 158). And in the final scene, there is that guttural, indescribable man noise.

In Italy, theorists involved in developing semiotic language included Umberto Eco, Emilio Garroni, Gianfranco Bettetini, Pier Paolo Pasolini; in France, Christian Metz, Roland Barthes and Félix Guattari; in the UK, Stephen Heath and Peter Wollen. Their collective work aims at critiquing the sense that any representation was 'natural' but they generally took the model for all languages to be speech (see Belsey 2002 for an account of this era). Roland Barthes' work on the theorisation of the image was a big influence to the debates of the second half of the twentieth century, as was the work of various localised film groups, and the theorisations around various 'new wave' cinemas that emerged in filmmaking communities, globally, at different times due to different circumstances (cf. Desser 1988; Cheuk 2008; Martin 2011). By 1970, however, Barthes had realised that it is not so much a focus on the components of signified and signifier, but an understanding of the organisation of signs, that will lead to comprehension of a system (see Barthes 1990b). With the exception of Wollen, who continued to develop a cultural semiology (see Wollen 1969, 2008) and Pasolini (who was murdered in 1975), Metz *et al.* are somewhat behind in their uptake of poststructuralist theories. Pasolini was interested in communicating material 'reality' at this time – a concern of many theorists who came up with semiological methods for screen analysis. As Guiliana Bruno (1991) has argued, much of Pasolini's work anticipates developments in post-structuralist theory. In his formative work, *Heretical Empiricism* (originally published in 1972), we find comments that do not quite fit with the prevailing sentiments and that would have not been out of place in the 'postmodern' debates of the late 1970s, in particular how he rails against the repressive controls of state and theologically endorsed controls over the individual. Pasolini constructed a 'general semiology' with which to account for 'the language of action, or in its simplest terms, of reality'

(2005: 204). Nevertheless, his approach to screen semiotics was discard by Metz and Eco. Metz commented: 'Pasolini had truly genial intuitions, but did not know how to formulate them on a scientific plane and this has discredited him among other semioticians' (cited in Viano 1993: 24). With his *Cinema 1* and *Cinema 2* works, Deleuze redirects attention to the value of Pasolini's semiology, particularly with the concept of 'free indirect discourse', that Pasolini developed from Bahktin (see Deleuze 1986: 74–6). Pasolini writes, 'Metz speaks of an "impression of reality" as a characteristic of film communication. I would say that it is a question not of an "impression of reality" but of "reality" itself ... The various real objects that compose a shot are the smallest unit of film language' (2005: 200). This is an example of grammatisation; an image-semiological approach (which Deleuze would utilise for his discussion of the components of the image) hotly contested in the film, art and literary theory journals of the early 1970s – including *Film Culture, Afterimage, Kinopraxis, Arts Yearbook, Screen, Artforum, Studio International* and *Tel Quel* – where we find the debates focusing on the physicality and materiality of the film processes, and a frustration and rejection of theories that seek to describe or ascribe 'meanings' from non-cinematic sources. Filmmakers such as Jean-Marie Straub, Glauber Rocha, Miklos Jansco, Pierre Clementi, Stan Brakhage and Michael Snow, and theorists including Regina Cornwell (1972), P. Adams Sitney (1971, 1974), Annette Michelson (1971) and Peter Gidal (1976, 1989) entered the debate regarding the tools of language with which to develop an expression of the materiality of film via the construction of the physicality of the analog film medium (celluloid film strip with chemical coating, sprocket holes and environmental residues of dust and grit, and so on) plus the semiotic debates of Metz (1974a) and Kristeva (1986). These deliberations involve what filmmaker Paul Sharits describes as the protocols of 'cinematics' (1972; for discussion on Sharit's Wittgensteinian interests see Leibman 1981: 3ff).

While these debates about the construction of the film sound and image as material signifier have been theorised before (eg. Kracauer's film theory of 'materialist aesthetics' from 1960; see also Hansen 1993), they are often absent from film theory work that overlooks its foremothers at the expense of constructing more nuanced argument. A return to the materialist debates of the 1970s is used in some but not all models in the 'new materialist' theory coming from race and gender studies, and is being picked up again by film theory (cf. Chare and Watkins 2012; De Bruyn 2012).

Theorised as the structural other of commercial, narrative films, pitted as a utopic savior against the attention economy produced by capitalist markets in which film participates, is the artisanal, or crafted, film work. While there are historical and technical reasons for this pairing, from theorists' writing in every era of film's production comes an attention to the definitions of the materials of film's own production as the semiology of film work, and as productive of an autonomous object; produced as an art form, with no commercial intent (for example the films of Len Lye). This is a modeling that, as Peter Wollen argues in a *Screen* article from 1975, broadly involves two senses of a materiality of film, which respond to Bazin's question, 'What is cinema?' There are conflicting answers to this (from theorists including Annette Michelson, Peter Gidal, P. Adams Sitney, various filmmakers and Wollen himself). There is the sense of the 'materials' of the film (its film, chemical production and screening) and the 'materiality' of the modes of production of the film (see Wollen 1976: 12).

As Wollen points out, there are many examples of textual and performative forms of discourse (from literary criticism, poetry) that already engage in the forms of deconstruction and rejection of any intentionality of 'a subject, a transcendental ego', 'a critique of illusionism' (1976: 19, 21). Wollen's call is to re-examine Bazin's ontological 'burden', where ascribing signification or 'meaning' of the world outside of cinema renders filmmaking as 'parasitic'. Instead, he argues for a de-realisation of 'the imaginary' and states that 'the material must be semioticised' (1976: 22). His position on the purpose of a materialist semiotic model differs from that put forward by the feminist-Marxist-materialist movement of the same time, which argued for a more applied understanding of the material requirements for life; for workers' bodies to sustain life, in order to feed capital (see Kuhn and Wolpe 1978: 7).

The materialist semiotic model for film involves describing the details of the material structure of cinema, and accounting for the processual nature of the image; one that is semiotically created, over time. This durational account of image-building is given other theoretical frames, and was described by Wollen, who cites Barthes' notion of *écriture* (writing) which enables 'seeing style as a blind force in comparison with writing marked as intentionality' (1975: 20, n.9). Less utopically stated than Wollen, filmmaker

Agnès Varda later developed this into her idea of a *cinécriture* (cinema writing) (see Smith 1998: 14; and Varda's film *Les Glaneurs et la glaneuse*, 2000), and a materialist aesthetic that continually asks the question of the cinematographic construction and production of a 'reality' that images display, engender or interrogate.

Re-examined in the context of the structuralist and feminist-materialist film theory produced post-1960s/1970s, Kracauer's 1960 thesis on the cinema as being 'materialistically minded' models a critical theory of vernacular materialism. This model appears in various forms, but with the same type of intent, across a broad spectrum of film theories that are usually looking to express something of a particular era, or grouping, a/ historical investigation, a perceived genre, thematic series, or particular technology of filmmaking – sound, cinematography, costume, set design, editing. Kracauer's conception of the material expression enabled by film – not just representation – but expression of a particular historical experience of 'the phenomenon of film' (Kracauer cited in Hansen 2012: 260), contributes to the 'affective turn' taken by film theorists such as Vivienne Sobchack (2004). Where investigation into the material phenomenon of film describe experience as operating as either embodied, or as part of the semiotic *écriture* of film theory, debates concerning affect as an experiential account extend into critical accounts of the normalisation of experience, and the normativity of bodies.

The materialist investigation runs through all films, necessarily, as the matter of life, as put into interaction with other matter connect to create situations, tensions, clashes, complementarity, and so on. While filmmakers of all kinds are very attendant to issues of materiality, film theories do not always emphasise the materiality of film, instead being interested with addressing the larger paradigmatic issues, such as 'representation', 'reality' and 'reconstruction'. In Sofia Coppola's *Marie Antoinette* (2006), the use of anachronistic materials (soundtrack and sneakers) providing extra-diegetic deconstructed material moments on screen, which were of pleasure to some theorists (for example, see Brevik-Zender 2011).

Writing on the use of voice-over narration in *Je tu il elle* (Chantal Akerman, 1974), Ivone Margulies notes: 'Through its abstractive powers, verbal language designates both small and large units of diegetic time – moments, days, the menstrual cycle. In its seemingly arbitrary connection to the visual track, it creates a sense of temporal abstraction' (1996: 115).

The opening title sequence, and title of the film, in Akerman's complex film about the predicated subject *Je, tu, il, elle* (I, you, he, her), lays out her title card with *her* at odds with the subject of other identity forms of subjunctive personal pronoun construction. Margulies writes that this film:

> proposes an instability between private and collective, internal and external, subject and object, author and character. The rift between the aural and the visual tracks in the film's first part suggests a gap between two formal logics that are suspended and made incongruous throughout the film. Indeed, *Je, tu, il, elle* procures less a shock of disjunction than an interstitial space between the disparate logics of abstraction and indexicality, anonymity and systems of nomenclature. (1996: 125)

Margulies's comments here provide a good summary of some of the key ways that film theory performs a modeling of film. This passage is taken from a book entirely on the topic of director Akerman's oeuvre. Titled *Nothing Happens*, the argument has a stated focus on the temporal and materialist content of Akerman's films, which Margulies reads in terms of the doubled meanings 'pairs', and counter points of the two 'logics'. These logics refer to many of the structural either/or images that Akerman's film logic builds. Margulies models her argument on the post-structuralist feminist theory of film (as practiced by the second-wave feminist theorists from the 1960s who examined iniquitous poser structures in everyday life for women [see Chaudhuri 2006: 4ff]), a position which critiques, as Anneke Smelik describes, 'how meaning [in the film] was acquired' (2009: 180). This theoretical position differs from that which describes film and film images as normative; a 'reflection of [a] meaning given in advance' (ibid.) Within a structural logic, often used in cognitivist film theory, time on screen where 'nothing happens' is sometimes argued in its most literal sense of the physical time of the 'action' or 'non-action' cinema. Mary Ann Doane uses this structural logic to suggest that in early film documentaries of 'real' events in time, the film displays 'dead time', as an indexical referent to the 'reality' of the image (2002: 140ff). Doane's argument re the 'destabilizing potential' (2002: 141) of cinematic time also can be read through the materialist lens, where she has constructed an architecture for extending the virtual play of the image (as we watch a film and the layers of meaning begin to build). Doane does this through the semiotic-vitalist philosophies of film argued by Deleuze and Bergson where time is theorised as not a chronological linear device but recognised as a spatialising encounter that film reveals, able to reorganise relations between things (see Deleuze 1986: 142ff; Bogue 2011; Colman 2011: 166ff; Mroz 2013: 191). The theorisation of screen duration, or filmic temporality, could fall into the semiotic or the materialist, depending on the approach (cf. Klevan 2000; Cua Lim 2009). As a time-based medium, film produces a performance of a specific materiality at a specific time, or as Margulies's subtitle for her book has it, a *hyperrealist everyday*.

Models of conclusion

As models of cognitive-semiotic theorisation headed down the pathways of explication of 'meanings' of the narratives that commercial films were telling, avant-garde practices were still engaged in examining the materialist implications of technologies of recording, reordering, sound production, image manipulation. The cognitivist and the materialist models highlight the issues at stake in film theory at this point; that being the comparison of artists', co-operative or independently-produced film, with the mainstream, commercially distributed film.

The aim of film theory is to produce an analysis of film, through words. This involves processes of compiling words, making lists, responding to images and sounds with expressive language that attempts to render the experience of watching or reflecting upon the experience, into language. Models, taxonomies, diagrams and systems suffuse film theory. Different theorists will describe the process of writing film theory in different ways. The writing of the theory is shaped by personal taste in film; aesthetic and thus political preferences. These aesthetic criteria determine the mode of engagement, disciplinary training, and other factors.

Modeling forms, technology, social issues, gender, nationality, race, sexuality, ethnicity, politics, ecological issues, the natural worlds, the imaginary worlds – as made by the film image – is not as straightforward as we think it might be. In the conceptualisation of the experience of the film image, film theory and philosophies of film are divided in their positions and opinions. As the platforms for film production shift and change, so too does language respond, modifying its expression of the experiences and knowledge of things in flux. Words mutate, disappear, fall foul of fashion or fads, or are claimed by certain groups and rejected by others. Language is a temporal form, like film; it is marked by its contextual era of use and like ideas, may be untimely in application. Film theory is a specific mode of discourse that has its own rules and regulations (creative to instrumental), and its grammar transverses a different technology (language) to the industry of film production (sound and image). Once distributed, films lose their proprietarily creative bubbles and become open texts, contributing and subject to the history and future of cinematographically conceived sound-images by their very modular nature. Once published, film theory's hermetic grammar is likewise subject to the history and future of cinematographically conceived sound-images as potential open source, sustainable grammars. Words and images are temporal objects, subject to political and economic drivers, historical interpretation and contextual narrativisation (see White 1973; Barthes 1976; Kristeva 1982). Linguistic platforms used by theory often ignore the material qualities of the matter under discussion (as in the chemical composition of cellulose triacetate plastic film strips, or the silver halide grains suspended in [animal-based] gelatin colloids of analog film), as scholarship on new materialism describes (Barad 2007; Alaimo and Hekman 2008; Chare and Watkins 2012). However, as film theory must situate the context of its words within a time-based, moving medium that involves different aspects as well as holistic notions of a spectator's body, as well as a film technology in order to produce its own model of linguistic expression, the transdisciplinary nature of the frameworks of film theory largely avoid the categorical errors of non-materialist theory.

Analysing and identifying the theoretical/generic/philosophic/material position of the screen text is a matter of using the appropriate methodology for expressive and polemic aims. But what is appropriate, given the range of modeling tools at our disposal? Each era in film theory has had a dominant methodology that we can retrospectively observe and critique. 'To build new models,' Janell Watson writes, 'is to build a new subjectivity' (2009: 9).

Notes

1   There are multiple examples, but just a few of the critical thinkers whose names are frequently referenced in film theorisation include the work on art by Rudolf Arnheim (1957), labour and work politics and Louis Althusser (1971), race and global politics by Stuart Hall (1989),

Etienne Balibar (1991) and Homi Bhabha (1983), cultural-philosophical models such as Gayatri Spivak on identity politics (1993), Judith Butler on performing gender (1993), Donna Haraway on technology (1991), Julia Kristeva on gender semiotics (1986).

2 In an article detailing the background to this episode, David Bordwell describes these events under the subheading of 'Bureaucracy VS the Avant-Garde' (see Bordwell 1972: 15; Eisenstein 1977); Dan Shaw discusses this episode (2008: 8–11); Warren Buckland comments on Bordwell's theoretical allegiance (2012a: 114–15).

3 Semiology is a science that studies the production of different signifying practices. Semiotic analysis, as applied to the theorisation of film, involves the study of cinema as a system of signs, where signifying practices engage certain types and styles of discourse that are able to be recognised, rejected and/or critiqued (cf. Wollen 1969; Metz 1974a; Stam *et al.* 1992; Buckland 2000b; Ehrat 2004).

4 The theory of language is called semiotics. This is the study of signs, that is something which stands for something else. In language, the word equals a signifier, which refers to the image/concept/thing equals signified. A sign equals a unity produced via a signifier and a signified. De Saussure's famous example is the chess board. If we have lost the black Queen, for example, we could still play the game if we both agree that we substitute another object, say a coin, that for the duration of the game will stand in for that Queen. So in De Saussure's system, a sign has value by virtue of its place in a system.

5 De Lauretis later expands her semiotic reading, and describes the site of the cinema screen in terms of a conglomerate of concepts about the signification of the image, via Kaja Silverman's use of Peirce's notion of iconicity, and the Lacanian mirror thesis (see De Lauretis 1987: 97ff).

6 For example, see Balázs 1970, 2010; Louis Delluc, cited in Abel (1988: 255–8); Ricciotto Canudo's collection of writing on film aesthetics, discussed in Rodowick (2014: 80).

2   TECHNOLOGY

As I shot, the structure of the film and the rhythm of the shoot-
ing emerged spontaneously from the landscape. The camera was
always moving through space; the visual imagery was constantly
in flux.
> – Nancy Holt, *Pine Barrens* (2011: 251)[1]

I was travelling on a spiritual mission, but sometimes I got distracted.
> – The Unborn Child, *Daughters of the Dust* (Julie Dash, 1991)

In *Cosmopolis* (novel by Don deLillo [2003]; film directed by David
Cronenberg [2012]), the character Vija Kinski, Eric Packer's 'Chief of Theory',
tells him that technology 'helps us make our fate'. This truism is given support in the narrative in a number of ways that hold the proposition to be
true. In Cronenberg's film, this dialogue takes place in one of the central
technology images of the film: the long white limousine, which is used for
the day by Mr. Packer (played by Robert Pattinson) as his mobile office.
As an example of automotive technology, in addition to its engineering
design for transportation, the limousine as this techno-image signals the
divergent histories of Fordist labour, and the automotive century's cultural
and economic structural divisions of visible and invisible, privileged and
disadvantaged, able and disabled, information and opacity. The vehicu-
lar technology Cronenberg's film expresses, reminds me of the political

(in the epistemic and economic terms of gendered, sexed, classed and racial) functions of *all technologies*. Technology, in its broadest sense, refers to the crafting or use of tools used to modify, create and craft materials to affect, interact or produce something. The automotive stage in *Cosmopolis* provided the situation for the digital camera (by Cronenberg's longtime Director of Photography, Peter Suschitzky), where one imagines the camera is guiding the action, and the highly restricted movement of that camera becomes the whole condition of the film, supplanted by the original soundtrack created by Cronenberg's composer Howard Shore and Canadian band Metric. It is the controlled, measured, electronic sounds of the end of one century.

As a field or paradigm for thinking about the image, 'technology' does not just refer to mechanical or digital things – such as the physical analog and digital equipment, the crafts involved in set, costume, make-up, storyboarding, chemical or digital processes required for pre- and post-processing, speed, timing and rhythms of editing, data storage, the technicalities of sound composition and recording, and so on. Technology also refers to all manner of ways in which the image is either mediated or autonomous – the either/or is contingent upon one's theoretical (or political) opinion on what kind of modeling affect technology has, or can have. And in that sense of mediation, and/or autonomy, comes restriction and control, as per *Cosmopolis*, which I described as a technology image. In Stiegler's terms, my description of the limousine as techno-image provides a grammatised image, where we understand the description a moving image's technological adaption through a written account of a number of connective technologies.

With changes in technology, new terms and neologisms come into play as the social and political materiality of technology affecting the way the film can be produced, and the ways in which theorisation might be adequate to those images are tested. When technology connects with sentient and other non-sentient beings, then new forms of political history are made – for example as we see played out in films like *Blade Runner* (Ridley Scott, 1982), where all beings desire the security given by what Arthur Krocker calls a 'genetic determinism' (2012: 122). Or, in *Dead Man* (Jim Jarmusch, 1995), where the town of Machine is a technological platform that facilitates the actions of its inhabitants through the genocide of one race in favour of another's industrial pursuits. There are films where historical technologies are staged, such as in *Jurassic Park* (Steven Spielberg, 1993) or *Free Radicals* (Len Lye, 1958–79). These different kinds of moments in film history are technologically-mediated events, created through specific material cultures, with specific sets of cultural knowledge and tools of technology. How does the film theory one writes respond to this mediation?

The type of technology used to make film determines the form of film that is made. This may seem like a redundant point to make, but it is both a structural and mediating condition – as well as component or device – that when highlighted or absented from film theory provides an immediate measure of what constitute the intentions and aims of the given theory. Without the electric current provided by a lightning bolt, Frankenstein's monster would not be given life. Different technologies enable different connections to be made. The operating systems of different technological platforms effectively present a system of formal boundaries (the space of the car; the open landscape) whereby the conditions for creativity emerge. For example, we see this in filmmaking industrial practices as bounded by strict national censorship laws, as in the case of Thailand or Australia, or formal technical rules concerning camera movement and the laws of physics – as in the case of Classical Hollywood cinema, or rules for the use of the DV digital video technology at the end of the 1990s by the *Dogme 95* group.

Collectively, societies do not yet know what technologies can enable. But we can speculate upon and test out their potential – collaboratively and individually. New technologies facilitate different practices, which in turn interface with resources, information and knowledge in new ways of conceiving of worlds, examining how they operate, and how the subjects and objects inside them operate, and what are their material forms. We can imagine and describe the possible consequences when we see the technology of an inanimate body irrigated by energy engage in processes that involve the sentient world. From the film producers' point of view, the value of this energised body is frequently in terms of its potential productive labour; how many entertainment units can *x* idea generate, or what is the profit return on a film, or its cultural value; its aesthetic (and thus political) potential, as a work of art or as a political manifesto. But from the film creators' position, there are other uses of technology. These may be built and programmed into the production, intuited and/or crafted through the technical tools available, and often filmmakers/cinematographers/ sound designers/visual designers will use a combination of approaches to achieve their image and film. The images that film technologies create are said to reflect, represent, copy, mirror, critique, question and embrace the 'reality' they have been drawn from. This type of position is critiqued for the value placed on the 'illusion' of the final (filmic, or media) image where the politics involved in technological crafting and design is ignored (see Kember and Zylinska 2012: 10) – for example, the discussion on the demands on human labour involved in the production of film (see Blair 2001). Theories that uncritically regard images as 'reflections' or 'representations' use already determined readings of their material cultures of production, given by an 'intergenerational' tertiary memory (see Stiegler 2010: 9). There are also theories that argue that technologies determine and mediate knowledge of 'reality', through means of the technological apparatus and its use (as described by Holt's guidance through space by the camera, reciprocating the movement of her gait through space).

In film theory, the address of the technologies of the cinema is uneven and sporadic. There is the technical manual, as in Barry Salt's work (2006, 2009), which is an empirical film theory as it is concerned with historical and technical details. But the technical details and their experiential testing and use *are* the language of the medium. So the discussion, for example, on the range of depth of field achieved by Gregg Toland's camera modification (see Cowan 2012), or why 'digital film' is an incorrect technicality (film strips are made of an unstable substance, celluloid, which record through chemical and light interface, whereas digital processes involve recording data) (see Streible 2013), or an anthropologist's field observations of the film production of a Tamali film crew turned speculative theory (see Pandian 2013) provide the material-semiotic details for all styles of film theory.

Film theorisation of film technology is limited, restricted in part by the theoretical preference for narrativisation. We see a film and want to respond to it as a story, as an experience to be described, telling how it affects us, the viewer, or what correlative allegories or metaphors about cultural, political and/or sociological issues it provides. In these senses, technology is but another model (as defined in the previous chapter); but it is necessarily – vis-à-vis the materiality of film – the meta-model that impacts upon all film theory. The experiential theorisation of new technologies dominates historical periods of technological innovation and change (cf. Elsaesser and Barker 1990; Schwartz 1995; Bennett *et al.* 2008; W. Brown 2013; Scholz 2013). How different people and generations respond to technological innovation is what will drive further investigation and testing of applications of technologies and their theorisation. Even if that is not the intention of all films, once distributed and in a public screening venue, interpretation is still of course mediated by the industrial factors that determine the senses of individuated subject and collective group, and access to theoretical models, and normative epistemologies that structure the experiences of those bodies.

Theorisations of technology are criticised for their commercially driven narrative of 'progress'; such as 'this camera is faster, smaller/ bigger/better' (for example, see Slane 1997: 72). The progressive narrative engages the modernist myth of technological 'solutions' to social and political problems, the naivety of the audience, and works through another political binarism of 'advanced/primitive' (cf. Gunning 1986; Russell 1999). Theoretical address of technology can wax lyrical about the 'freedom' it promises to the 'imagination', but ignore the ways in which the fetishisation of technologies have led to the exploitation of workers (see Beller 2013), the depletion of natural resources (see Bozak 2011), changes to images of sex on screen (see White 2006: 174), the mediation of desire, and so on. Direct technical address of the medium was at first contingent upon access to films and film technology (cf. Whannel and Harcourt 1964: 5–7). Usually there is a separation in film theory between those that directly address how something works, and those that ignore the technology altogether. It is common to pick up a film theory book and find no reference to technology or the technological in the text of the book, index, notes or research references. In writing, it is often assumed that the specialist reader of film theory *knows* that the technological platform has been crafted and designed in order to achieve its results. On the other hand, theories that model their analysis and thesis upon the technological platform types are routinely subject to critiques of 'technological determinism', where the argument claims that technology is what determines society and culture – including the cultural artefacts it produces, such as film. The correlative position to this is technological autonomy, claiming that technology develops through its own logic, and is not something that humans control (Dusek 2006: 84). These positions are notions that films and film theory frequently test (cf. Virilio 1989; Kellner 1999; Stiegler 2011; Scholz 2013), and are taken further in critical media theories that address technology in cultural and political terms (for example, Haraway 1991; Grau and Veigl 2011).

In film theory, the term *technology* is used in a number of different ways, as per the theory. For example, De Lauretis's (1987) *technologies of gender* on screen have a different contextual meaning than Stiegler's sense of *filmic technology* as a prosthetic for human memory and conscious-ness (2011: 60). Yet there are connections to be made and distinctions to be drawn between the writing of technological platforms that produce content. In film theory, attention to the technology of the production of the film – the materiality of the filmic content – is not always in evidence. Nonetheless the technological platform always contributes to the determi-nation of the distributed meaning.

For clarity (and economy), in this chapter I approach the multiple theo-retical approaches to technology by film theory for their focus on distinc-tive facets of cinema. The core types are (i) *industrial practices*, where theory constructs arguments concerning the movements and histories of film technologies; and (ii) *the matter of mediation*, where theory addresses the materiality of film technology in aesthetic-political, critical, conceptual and philosophical terms. By way of conclusion, this chapter raises a third point, the theoretical elephant of a technologically facilitated 'reality' in and by film theory. While these three approaches are not exclusive, they are easily distinguished by methodological approaches, where the account of film creation is informed by its discipline specific rules, or broken rules as in the case of transdisciplinary writing, and the cultural mores of gram-matisation.

Industrial practices and im/materialflows
On 17 January 2014, at 3:47pm, *The Los Angeles Times* reported that the Hollywood film studio, Paramount Pictures had stopped releasing movies on analog film formats in United States theatres (see Verrier 2014). 35mm film projection was the format used in cinema theatres since its invention and first screenings at the start of the twentieth century in New York (see Gomery 1992: 34ff). This fact is significant in terms of the dominance that analog filmic industrial practice held for the first century of filmmaking, as the industry moves to all-digital film global releases by the Hollywood stu-

dios (Paramount's first all-digital release was Martin Scorsese's *The Wolf of Wall Street*, 2013). As I read this headline about Paramount, I can almost hear the cheers of glee from the experimental filmmakers and the graves of the historical avant-garde filmmakers ringing in at that exact moment. Jonas Mekas did not hold back when he wrote:

> Hollywood films (and we mean Hollywoods all over the world) reach us beautiful and dead. They are made with money, cameras, and splicers, instead of with enthusiasm, passion, and imagination. If it will help us to free our cinema by throwing out the splicers and the budget-makers and by shooting our films on 16mm as Cassavetes did, let us do so ... there is no other way of breaking the frozen cinematic ground than through a *complete* derangement of the official cinematic senses (1971: 75)

Mekas's refusal of the commercial narrative cinema's interests is indicative of the theoretical divide in aesthetic and political positions, between commercial and art-film practices. The structure of this apparent oppositional, reactionary stand-point offers an antagonistic reciprocity, as commercial films learn techniques and ideas from the experimental, thus lending awareness and tolerance of the terms of avant-garde experimentation (see debates in Michelson 1971; Cornwell 1972). Often, a (false) equilibrium is reached between the two, as commercial practices absorb the experimental, while the innovations of an artistic practice struggle to compete against commercially-funded industries' applications of technologies that facilitate, produce and distribute innovations in image- and sound-making faster than independent companies. So we see in commercial narrative cinemas the use of previously experimental-only techniques. The absorption of the marginal by the mainstream is one of capital's cyclical traits, where information and ideas, and creativity flows from one circuit of production to another, losing some of the context and material specificity on the way.

Mekas's own style of filmmaking produced personal films, poetically structured, engaging in what Naficy terms the epistolary mode (2001), a style commonly seen in exilic filmmaking, but always in pursuit of the medium itself. An obsession with technology and its possibilities, and its restrictions (as Mekas points out above, sarcasm notwithstanding), has produced a significant, although small, body of film theory devoted to the artist film, manifesto-style philosophies of film technology (for example, see Sitney 1971; Gidal 1976, 1989; O'Pray 2003; Curtis 2007; Speilmann 2008). Together with Jerome Hill, P. Adams Sitney, Peter Kubelka and Stan Brakhage, Mekas was one of the co-founders of the Anthology Film Archives in New York, in 1969. This archive collects and exhibits forms of film that are made as art.[2] The stated intention of the archive is to 'encourage the study of the medium's masterworks as works of art rather than disposable entertainment' (*Anthology Film Archives* 2014).

Mekas's group is an example of a well-organised artists' collective, devoted to not just the practice but also the archiving of their technology. In the 1960s the first portable video cameras (albeit with suitcases full of batteries) enabled new modes of independent filmmaking practices, not only in New York, from where Mekas speaks, but globally, situated in specific locales. The same era, for example, would see develop in the UK a group of what is historically known as British expanded cinema. Less formal 'groupings' were provided with theorisation and validation of the terms of a 'materialist cinema' of the late 1970s, through practitioners Peter Gidal and Malcolm Le Grice, described as oppositional to the main-stream dominance of narrative commercial film (see Gidal 1976; Le Grice 2001; Ball 2011: 272). These positions have been critiques for their lack of address of feminist filmmaking issues of the 1970s era of their produc-tion (see De Bruyn 2012: 89), for example, in the now fairly well-known filmic works of the same era – such as those by Carolee Schneeman, Marie Menken and Yoko Ono (see Mellencamp 1990: 21). Artists' filmmaking col-lectives also engage a different set of work practices, in part determined by their relationship with the technologies they use, in comparison to the restricted, economic requirements of workers that produce the Hollywood technological machinery of film, where Fordist work practices make enor-mous demands on human labour.[3]

Technological changes are mapped out in film theory against, or com-paratively with changes in resourcing costs. These are contingent upon the local economic and governmental concerns. The terms of the continuous economic restructuring of the twentieth-century Hollywood production studios (see Balio 2013) is a now historical account of the local events with global impacts. In addition to recounting the events, some film theorisa-tion also looks to analyse its local use of new technologies and what their economic infrastructure does for the film industry. For example, Ranjani Mazumdar argues that the ways in which the various Bollywood production companies organise their star's bodies, through technological facilitation, has produced 'a new language of liveness' (2012: 835). The *liveness* of technological mediation is something that all media forms have used to spatialise their experience of technology and the self-referentiality of technology, as it contributes to the work being made (art films whose work is about the physicality of making work, such as *One Plus One* [Jean-Luc Godard, 1968]; commercial films about the process of making a film such as *Singin' in the Rain* [Stanley Donen and Gene Kelly, 1952]). However, the theorisation of 'liveness' is also itself subject to criticism for its assumptions about what and who constitute that 'life' (cf. Stiegler 2011: 64, 68; Kember and Zylinska 2012: xvi).

In theorising technology and film, cinema and screen images, the terms of the materiality and physics of movement are employed – for example, in the writing of issues of territory, space, duration, velocity and determination of content, spatialisation. In her modeling of the affects to perception of the world via satellite technologies, Lisa Parks describes televisual information in terms of technological modes of 'convergence' as a 'relational model of understanding how technologies inflect, inform, and interact with one another in the process of their emergence' (2005: 77). She describes the structure of technological convergences (and we could think of other forms of convergence here, for example between the gaming industry and film, or between the porn industry and commercial cinema and so on), in terms of 'a form of horizontal fragmentation (or flow) but also as a set of vertical practices of uplinking and downlinking' (2005: 69). Parks' terminology of verticality is drawn from Deleuze, and invokes a question of territoriality and the differences between striated and smooth spaces (see Deleuze and Guattari 1987: 482ff). The term 'flows' is described by cultural theorist Arjun Appadurai as a series of global flows of ideas and cultural materials that media forms facilitate across the globe, but often resulting in strangely apolitical manifestations of imagery and ideas (see 1996: 29–30).

Appadurai describes how global flows operate to create a placeless 'community', full of 'ironies and resistances' as they share images but not cultural or political affinities (1996: 29). His example concerns how 'nostalgia without memory' can occur in cultures, which we often see in 'post'-

media forms that draw from a history or place never experienced. Parks provides a good example of where technological forms facilitate a shift in cultural memory – without the physicality of experience – through the lines of flow or linkage between convergent media. Parks describes how a 1999 videotaped story on the Australian Indigenous 'Stolen Generation' by an Imparja TV camera operator, Dwayne Ticker, was picked up from the local Yuendumu Imparja National News by commercial Australian television networks, then CNN, and then via satellite, globally distributed (2005: 68–9). The results of which was an Australian filmmaker living in New York, Phillip Noyce, seeing this news item and deciding to make a film about this aspect of Australian history, *Rabbit-Proof Fence*.[4]

The theorisation of the role of technologies in convergences of cultures has been mapped in a number of different ways by film theory. First, it looks at adaptations of different technologies of print media, commonly from news stories, scripts, poetry, novels, photographs and art images. Convergences between film and other disciplines also occur, as a sharing of technological platforms of information, such as the translation of ideas, discoveries and stories from the sciences and other humanities, narrativised and imaged (see Jenkins 2006; Brown and Krzywinska 2009: 91). Convergences between film and other technological forms (such as robotics) have historicised technological events as contributing to larger media archaeologies at work across cultures (cf. Ellul 1967; Elsaesser 2004; Ndalianis 2006; Parikka and Hertz 2010), and the grammatisation process in filmic worlds, or cinematic 're-producibility' (Stiegler 2011: 213–15).

The matter of mediation

What these (and other) theories of instances of convergences of film forms and cultures direct critical theorisation to is a consideration of the implications of filmic technology and the grammatical terms of historical medium materiality. The territorial privilege of technology and its display in terms of film also draws theoretical attention. The question of access to materials is as significant to the theoretical ability to connect with the materiality of the experience. Sometimes this connection has unexpected consequences. So I will take examples from a few different film forms to discuss – first an ethnographic film, a detour back to a narrative experimental film, then a brief look at animation in this chapter, and a narrative cinema in the following chapter, then we begin to see how film theory describes the filmmaker-as-technological body's privilege of access as deterministically bound with progress narratives or ethical questions.

Filmmaker Jean Rouch conceptualised the idea of Dziga Vertov's *Cinéma vérité*, described by Bill Nichols as an 'observational cinema' (1991: 108ff). Rouch's access to Songhay West African rituals enabled him to theorise the technological platform of his camera for a range of reasons (see Russell 1999: 218–21). It is these reasons that draw attention to Rouch's work, and how film theory treats the question of cine-mediation. Most accounts of the histories of observational cinema will mention in passing Rouch's technique and aims, linking his work with Edgar Morin, as they worked together on projects. However, while some film theory accepts the work that Rouch did uncritically, some eulogise his work (see Stoller 1992), others will point to the questionable ethics of his films, and their theorisation (see Russell 1999: 228), which were a result of the mediation of the camera technology. Roach states that he used his camera to 'seek the truth', couched in the historical endorsement of Vertov' *kinopravda* – literally meaning the 'film truth' of the camera, where film would not show any kind of 'staged reality', but capture life 'unawares' (Petrić 1993: 4). Rouch described his version of *kinopravda* as '*cinétranse*', where the filmmaker leaves his body (as in a trance) and becomes one with the camera equipment, able to record the 'pure truth'; the technologised 'reality' that 'only the camera' can see (Russell 1999: 77ff)

Vlada Petrić argues that the contradictions inherent in Vertov's approach are to be seen within the context of his historical milieu; that of a constructivist aesthetic that used deconstructive methods in order to reconstruct 'the truth' (1993: 10ff, 188; see also Aitken 2002: 57–8). Catherine Russell cautions against reading Rouch too literally, or out of his historical context (1999: 228). The integration of technology and 'man' may come through the mediation of themes and genres; for example, religious technologies that allow the discussion of the camera-Rouch-body as a 'shaman' (Michael Eaton cited in Russell 1999: 228). There is also the discussion of the camera-body as anthropomorphised actor, where technology performs: 'By virtue of its material form and technological apparatus, cinema wears its performative intervention openly' (Bell 2007: 4). Following this logic we can describe Rouch's 'truth' as performing a semiotic-ritual, to which we can also add the technological structuring devices of editing, cuts, frame matches, the cognitive figuring of a rhythm of relations (see Bordwell 1985: 76). As Lev Kuleshov noted: 'A shot must be treated like a sign, like a letter' (cited in Drummond *et al.* 1979: 4).

Can technology ever capture the world? Desires? Ideas? Imagination? Specters? Death?

Theories abound where cinema is described as a mixing of art and technology (see Blassnigg 2009). We can speculate, as Julie Dash does in *Daughters of the Dust,* as to what the technology of the camera might be able to register; to perceive that which the human eye cannot perceive. In this film, ancestral figures of the past and future take the forms of spectral children and the earthly elements, and the food consumed, the physical rituals followed, the winds, the seas, the earth, and the senses are all given equal attention within the film world's *mise-en-scène*. Several kinds of technology are deployed as motifs in the film, used as devices that signal the recording and the re-ordering of the past and the mortal duration of those present; buttons, fabric. This is the spectral vitality of film that Barthes and Bazin sought to describe in their writing about the image – photographic and moving. There is the technology of food, of indigo dye for cotton production, technologies of witchcraft and of photography. Jacqueline Bobo describes Dash's use of technology as a homage, which 'establishes a creative provenance' for the film (1995: 133). Bobo describes the production and meanings of the film scenes and narrative layers through a historical account of each image's provenance – the use of the large-format camera is a reference to the Harlem photographer James Van der Zee. Bobo's account of technologies as layers of motifs describes a sensorial grammatisation as a power that their visualisation holds. Bobo's theory echoes the script's aim of the 'empowerment of black women' (1995: 165). Bobo suggests that the technology that has enabled the image to realise its potential also becomes a tool of interrogation of the image itself.

Consideration of the apparatus of the cinema, and of film, has led theory to a number of surprising places. Apparatus theories of the 1970s and 1980s focused on either metaphorically relating the visual field to psychoanalytic theories (see Baudry 1986; De Lauretis and Heath 1986), or the audio field to a semiotic-psychological model (see Doane 1985; Bonitzer 1986), or to the philosophical field (see Lyotard 1986; Silverman 1986) or gender model (see De Lauretis 1986). In the face of digital developments, at first glance, this era's focus on psychoanalytic models and use of psychoanalytic terminology seems hopelessly narrow and out of touch with filmmaking practices and, as I discuss in the following chapter, a few key theories unfortunately make generalist statements about a universal 'spectator' that can alienate/exclude other spectators. However, some of the arguments are well worth closer analysis for their contribution to debates on semiotics, materialism, affect, and can be read in positivist ways for their highlighting of areas where theoretical and practical work needs to be done.

Apparatus theories use analogy and metaphor to relate the physical experience of a screen projection to the spectator, and the image is described in terms of positive or negative attributes (the lack, the look, the gaze). Psychoanalytic modeling ascribes gender, sex and racial roles to screen images, so putting those politics aside for a moment we are left with the still binarist terms of a historical piece of technology. Thinking purely in terms of a specific apparatus will lead film theory to ascribe the terms of 'old' and 'new media' (as Lev Manovich defined in 2001). Some of the apparatus theoretical positions, however, developed into different strands. Thinking about time and sound, for example, but also taking on the technological determinist challenge of thinking about the actual *ontology*; the being of the camera as autonomous.

Unlike the dominant film theorists of the 1980s, Donna Haraway's prescient comment in her *Cyborg Manifesto* (from 1984) states: 'The machine is not an it to be animated, worshipped, and dominated. The machine is us, our processes, an aspect of our embodiment' (1991: 180). If the machine is 'us' as the camera then how do the differences in technology affect this processual body? As a nineteenth-century industrial invention, the camera measured light photons. The construction of analog film worlds is done by light energy, harnessed into photochemical film. Digital images are constructed through the light entering the camera's lens, which focuses the light (tone and duration) onto electronic sensors where individual charges convert light into digital data pixels. The digital has shifted the possibilities of image production. The aesthetic of the image has altered, although post-production effects can achieve something of the analog's silver halide crystals, the depth of the image is different between digital and analog. The digital is not just about coding and computation. Just like analog film, the digital is used as a visual creative tool, as a platform technology for generating content. Unlike analog, the digital has created new archival possibilities for both old and new media forms. Cinematographers, editors and post-production workers all have to be attendant to the new and unknown aspects of the digital; there are many stories about technicians building their own systems. Because digital is a malleable recording device that translates light and sound into zeros and ones then there is no degradation of that information in the editing room (which happens with photochemical film) as it is taken out, manipulated, reordered, augmented, put back into pixel plastic strips (see Fossati 2014). So the digital film system as we know it today exists as a result of the technical skills and creativity of studio technicians, as well as the larger production vision. Many texts exist on film techniques, how to light/shoot/edit (see, for example, Murch 2001). Film theory *per se* has not yet figured a way to accommodate the pragmatics with the materialist, with the desire to tell stories about favourite films. How to be an artist and a film technician at the same time is what is missing from film theory scholarship. For example, the history of how George Lucas built his own technology company so that he could film the kind of worlds he imagined on screen require some critical contextualising, while at present we have either press release promotional materials from Lucas's company (see Block 2010), or passing references in philosophy of film texts (see Wilson 2013); neither of which are inaccurate, but connected would provide a more nuanced account. Haraway's machine theory thus posits us as camera, as a dynamic technology. Theorisation of the processes of machinic 'embodiment' of the processes of cinematography have produced speculation on the perceptual capacities of humans as structured by machinic potentia, perhaps more fully realised in film than in theory as yet (cf. *Videodrome*, David Cronenberg, 1983).

The archiving of film images has drawn much attention in film theory due not only to the implications that a realisation of preservation or destruction achieves (see Cherchi Usai 2001; Fossati 2014), but has also highlighted the potential within the archive (see Parikka and Hertz 2010) that builds with information, coding and digitised knowledge. The modeling of the archive, informatics and new digital technologies redirect attention to the languages and codes of cinematic grammar. The terms of 'obsolescence' for industrial technologies like film, forms the subject of many films (for example, *Disappearance at Sea* by Tacita Dean [1996]; see discussion by Connolly 2009: 53), and film theory has turned to the ways in which data might be preserved through digital means that bypass the physical deterioration of the film strip.

The onset of the digital for commercial film has seen analog technologies receive more attention for their novelty factor, for the question of what technology can animate and for their aesthetics. From the 1950s the influence of television on film production marked a shift in technologies and in the grammatisation of images, through the availability of the VCR from the 1980s (see Friedberg 1993: 132). From the 1960s, artists' films (including 16mm film projection) and videos (NTSC, PAL, SECAM), once minor forms in art galleries, became more visible. Access to the Internet from the end of the 1990s enabled access to both art and commercial film (analog and digital), video and other screen-based media. The change from analog to digital technologies and accessibility to the Internet at the end of the 1990s caused a further re-direction of the technology image. In 2014, the British Broadcasting Corporation (BBC) has a whole department devoted to 'Future Media' which investigates the spectator's interactive potential, with the 'red button' of home viewers' remote control providing real-time feedback to 'live' broadcast services.

The availability of digital technology for filmmaking had a restricted moment over the turn of the century. The first fully digital films were in theatres in the late 1990s, distributed under 'art-house' guise. Two independent companies capture the global market's attention with their digital films: the first is the New York-based company InDigEnt (Independent Digital Entertainment). The second are those made by Zentropa, based in Hvidovre, Denmark.[5]

The InDigEnt films have thus far received far less critical or theoretical attention than their Danish cousins. At the 2001 'digital film festival' at ACMI (The Australian Centre for the Moving Image) I saw Bruce Wagner's *Women in Film* (2001), which provides an acerbic commentary on the Hollywood industry. Taking the digital as its platform (recording devices are a constant motif), the film uses black humour to engage the nature of experimental filmmaking, and as the title suggests, it tackles the issue of 'women in film', onscreen, as support industries (masseuse, wife, lover, prostitute, producer, psychologist, hired help, mother), in terms of their colour, class and ethics. Produced by Pam Koffler, Jon Marcus and Christine Vachon (who produced most of Todd Haynes' work, including *Superstar: The Karen Carpenter Story* [1987] and Cindy Sherman's *Office Killer* [1997]), *Women in Film* follows Pasolini's lead in *Theorem*, first in building images through small units, each emphasising the (digital) cinematographic recording process, and second through the conceit of one of the stories within the film as a systemic process, that of a Hollywood producer (played by Beverly D'Angelo), trying to raise funds to do a remake of *Theorem*. Sound binds the otherwise schizo film together, images are edited to the soundtrack of instrumental songs from Boston-based indie band The Supreme Dicks; Mozart's death march, 'Requiem'; and the women actor's confessional monologue and singing. The producer's funding for the *Theorem* remake becomes stalled, however, as she has an (unsighted, but narrated) affair with her future lead actor.

InDigEnt did venture into more commercial films (such as *Pieces of April* [Peter Hedges, 2003]), but was not successful in terms of technological innovation at the time (see Willis 2005: 32). The *Dogme 95* rules of DV and hand-held camera restricted the use of equipment and after effects, producing a specific style that was globally copied and has since become synonymous with that technological moment (see Hjort and MacKenzie 2003: 164). The digital capture of sensory and movement data in the real-time of the body's interaction with the world signal another shift in the breadth of cinematographic perceptual embodiment, as the cinematographers of *Cosmopolis* and of *Festen* (the first *Dogme* film, directed by Thomas Vinterberg, DoP Anthony Dod Mantle, 1998) comment in their production notes. A rethinking of the technical possibilities of filmmaking as a digital ecology create new forms in cinematography. The disappearance of 35mm film material enables new forms to emerge, as different technical platforms are tested. As much as analog practices continue to inform some styles of filmmaking, including processes such as those seen in the 3D conversion work of commercial films like *Gravity* (Alfonso Cuarón, 2013), filmmakers are pursuing different agendas for filmmaking.

Theorisation of innovations in digital technology tend to be either auteurist (fascinated by the director Lars von Trier, for example; see Stevenson 2002), critical of the technical conceit of the rules of the model for theorisation that repeats the same lineage histories of film theory (see Thanouli 2013), or just summative of events. As Philip Cowan (2012) points out, the modeling of film theory around the name of the director, or theories of auteurship, has a serious flaw in logic, as filmmaking is a largely collaborative practice, and the technical contribution of various people misses the creative and material elements of that process in its theorisation. In other words, although film theory convention currently dictates the use of the director's name as the 'author' of the film, filmmaking is a collaborative effort, whether in the use of materials created by others, or in the use of a film crew. Although it relies on standard notions of crafting the set and actors, discussion of the film *Gravity* provides a new paradigm for the theorisation of the expanding role of the cinematographer on films with significant virtual components. This role was noted in discussion of Cuarón's work in *Children of Men* (2006), which incorporated innovative filming techniques to attain a 'new' standard of filmic 'realism' for the time of production (see Amago 2010). In film theory, the film narrative has been addressed, less so the implications of the use of digital technology (see Chaudhary 2009). Cinematographer Emmanuel Lubezki and visual effects supervisor Tim Webber worked closely with the director (see Benjamin 2013; especially the workflow chart that details the technical steps in the production of this film). The digital recording of light proved to be one of the tricks for setting continuity and making textual depth. Because this is a film set in orbit around the Earth, the mimicry of that position in space was achieved in many technical ways, including through 'the programming of lighting environments that would mimic the filmed bodies' (ibid.) at given times of their orbit (breakfast over Mexico, sunset over camera-movement trajectories and for both characters' points of view).

The technical roles in filmmaking are many, including the cinematographer, sound designer, the visual-effects supervisor, set designer, props, wardrobe, stunt doubles, and so on. Criticism of the lack of theoretical attention to the role of technicians (such as Cowan 2012) takes a different form in discussion of artist's films, where the filmmaker is often the director, editor, cinematographer and actor. Also the artist film often contains a rhetorical expression, presenting itself as a modernist- or materialist-styled manifesto about the nature of the work of film, being about the investigation into film's material conditions or situation, including the 'failures' of technology.[6] Technological processes, as told in terms of the 'progression' narrative of technology, with 'theory' and 'history' conveyed is the domain of commercial film (see *Side By Side* [2012], a documentary produced by Keanu Reeves which 'explains' the technological changes in significant commercial film moments). Questioning why theorists and critics of film kept proclaiming it [celluloid film] 'dead' with the proliferation of digital in the early 2000s, Jonathan Walley notes that far from being 'dead', artists who continue to use [analog and digital] film in their expanded cinema practices of filmmaking, installation and performance have moved past the 'pure film-specific research' and its 'jettisoning of meaning' and this form of cinema's current investigations 'restores meaning to a highly material cinema' (2011: 250). The question of the 'value' of a 'content' that is external to the film's technological properties is not noted by Walley, but the list of 'content' he gives is what you do see at any current selection of artist's films in galleries: 'analogies with nature, the organic, the body, references to film history, politically-charged distinctions between film and video, even illusionism and visual pleasure' (ibid.). Walley names classifiable positions, each of which come attached with identity politics. Examples of such positions are to be found in other and earlier materialist films including the work of Stan Brakhage, Len Lye, Carolee Schneeman, Maya Deren, Nancy Holt, Richard Serra, Liz Rhodes, Derek Jarman and Malcolm Le Grice.

Temporal mediation, and its failures
The use of a technology in film, or film theory, is not always given as a progressive utopic narrative, nor is it always solely concerned with material factors. Disenchanted with the way that Hollywood uses its technicians, Theodor Adorno and Hanns Eisler wrote a scathing account of their experiences in composing for Hollywood films during the classical period:

> In motion picture music, the idea of the whole and its articulation holds absolute primacy, sometimes in the form of an abstract pattern that conjures up rhythms, tone sequences, and figures at a given place without the composer's specific knowledge of them in advance. (1994: 95)

Adorno and Eisler's concern with the conditions for [creative] work, and the worker's conditions and rights appear, ironically enough in another instance of convergence through grammatisation.[7] Speculating on the queer content of computer-generated imgery such as the animated Pixar films' including *Finding Nemo* (Andrew Stanton and Lee Unkrich, 2003) and *Chicken Run* (Peter Lord and Nick Park, 2000), Judith Halberstam argues the Pixar films are preoccupied with 'revolt, change, cooperation, and transformation' (2011: 79), and are not only subversive, but offer queered social models where workers can reorganise themselves into a collaborative model of work and shared labour.

Animation as a film technology has always presented for film theory instances of what I call a *materialist media grammatisation*, where relational a connections are formed between multiple types of media and recording information – graphic, symbolic, analog, digital, different audio tracks, and multiple movement techniques, post-production methods and conditions of work for the studio required to produce the labour-intensive animated cells or frames. Of course the details of the materiality are in how theory is addressing the type of production of the images, whether in Mickey Mouse in *Steamboat Willy* (Ub Iwerks and Walt Disney, 1928), *Spirited Away* (Hayao Miyazaki, 2001) or *Chicken Run*.

Referring to the production of the intensive Japanese *anime* industry Thomas Lamarre (2009) refers to both the technology of animation (the multiplane camera that Walt Disney invented), and the development of *otaku* psychology through the popularity of *anime* cultures, as the 'animetic machine'.[8] In both Halberstam and Lamarre's approaches, the technological materiality of production is treated as the grammatisation machinery, where psychology, and political ideology is connected to this production to critique the film image. These are examples of a theory of technology that is neither solely deterministic, nor sees the machine as autonomous, but is reliant on engaging with the local crafting of materials and ideas to design and realise the film. The materials of film perform as temporal objects within their cinematic systems of making.

With the creation of images, the forms of technology used will influthe activity of the image. We see different types of image performance facilitated from different film technologies, and this determines in part the modes of acting (of things and of all living organisms, not just people) that can take place within the diegetic world, and as this image contributes and is mediated by the lived world. An analog film reel has a determinate time-limit that actors and crew work to, compared with the unlimited digital recording time of a scene. Thus what is written or conceived of as a ten-minute scene to be shot on 35mm requires a thousand feet of celluloid film in the reel, with digital, the limitation of scene time is given also through data storage capacity, but this is more easily solved than the physical requirements of chemical film processing. Thus digital modes of production of images can extend for days and weeks of filming in order to get the 'right' performance recorded. What the intensification that the digital enables – through both performance (for example, see the reviews for Lars von Trier's *Nymphomaniac* [2014]) – and through change in the speed and volume of 'frames' (see Bordwell 2002; Shaviro 2010) is not the concern of this chapter, although the (aesthetic and thus political) activities enabled by this intensification arise as an implicit question for this reader.

In terms of performance and film, it is always worth remembering Kuleshov's theory, that technically the cinema is a language working with units. To think of this theory, made in the analog-only era but perfectly translatable as an element of the grammars of technology, is to imagine a new vocabulary for film theory. Digital platforms enable different types of transformation of matter, and this is the commonality we see across all digital ecologies. Using methods of copying, compression, deviation, granularity and synchronisation, the digital has transformed the ways that we understand and interact with data, materials, designing and aestheticising the world. New types of modeling software and hardware has enabled architects, artists, designers, filmmakers and theorists to create forms that would have been unimaginable or very difficult to produce by using traditional methods. Contingent upon their theoretical intention, film theory describes this change in form in the terms of its queering; its making different, or making new, or its redirection. The writing of the forms as produced by a specific material mediation provides the content, expressed affectively and or technically.

Let us go a little closer in reading the images with the performance of technologies model to see how the convergences flow. Lamarre's machinic affect of *anime* is drawn from the language of Félix Guattari, who wrote of machines and models (see 1995; 2012). In performing the technologically enhanced body, a machinic affect (of the specific technology) occurs. The body may be enhanced by its acted gestural styles, by make-up, by costuming, or with prosthetics, all providing readymade effects. In *Holy Motors* (Leos Carax, 2012), for example, multiple prostheses are used to imitate and animate the various acts of the film. The bodies of the actors perform their various roles through their material enhancements, with Carax directing an overplay of the dramatisation of the body. These technologies of disguise are what the film centres upon, as with materialist cinema of the 1960s and 1970s. The film work is the work. Characters in *Holy Motors* perform multiple possibilities for the filmic body of 2012, and are cast in a very different way from Cronenberg's cosmopolitan futurist machine. We can literally read the 'Holy Motors' as the anthropomorphised machinic body (or 'soul' machine, after Lamarre [2009: 200]), as these limousines are fully cogniscant of their impending obsolescence. Human bodies that pass through the motors are recognisable by their performance of a specific technology of gender (to appropriate De Lauretis's terminology), they are in a range of disguises, including performing in motion-capture suits, rendered as *anime* game avatars. In one scene, the enhancement of the reconstructed *Pietà* with costuming and penile prosthesis points to a consideration of the performance of the prosthetic effects of life as technology images of material processes.

Film theorists will address the durational concept in terms of its technological platform in various ways. The medium of electricity provides the common language for two films that Mary Ann Doane describes, Actuality films (short films of everyday life) that are 'indexical' records of time that nevertheless display certain unassimilable' incidents (2002: 140). The tightly orchestrated structure of the film sequences, Doane argues, engage the historical modes of history event/disaster paintings and photography, where the everyday details and contingencies exceed the formal staging of the image (see 2002: 142–43). Doane's examples include the 'actualities', recordings of live events such as the reenactment of the electrocution of the man that killed US President McKinley in 1901, *Execution of Czolgosz with Panorama of Auburn Prison* (Edwin S. Porter, 1901) and the infamous *Electrocuting an Elephant* (Thomas A. Edison, 1903). Doane reads these films through their empirically observed structure, and duration, for analysis that uses some of the technological factors but remains more speculative in the modeling of the event of death/s on screen.

In technical terms, film duration dictates what will make the final cut and what is discarded in editing. In theoretical terms, time is an abstract concept, so the screen image must work to provide both form and content for this abstraction. It does so in a number of ways; (i) time on screen is expressed as a spatialised concept (as an event, a place, a song, perhaps a map or expression of the variations of life, self-reflexive screen forms or as a film within a film); (ii) chronometric and durational time is given form through various themes (the unchanging forms of daily life, generational change, the movement of physical things, essences, ideas, and their material and existential tendencies); (iii) time is imagined as an expression of other dimensions of life (experiential moments, essences without physical presence, spiritual senses, memories, hallucinations, dreams, recollections, *deja-vu*). Describing the story of *Eternal Sunshine of the Spotless Mind* (Michael Gondry, 2004) Chris Dzialo denotes the action as 'the struggle against the endless erasure of projector time' (2009: 116) – a phrase that could be used to summarise a few very significant aspects of twentieth-century cinema technology: the end of the projector as a grammatisation of the materials of duration – brains, bodies, time, projector.

When technological materials converge through film to record (as in the actualities or in documentary film), or to create new images, theory can describe this as a 'contingency within [filmic] structure' as Doane does (2002: 171). Or, theory can take a philosophical view, and use the notion of 'presentism' (see Cox and Levine 2002: 102–3) to try to express the experience of the passage of time that Doane also struggles to express. But many film theories that look at time today do not write in terms of the singular viewer's experience, and in fact put forward theories that are irreducible to any notion of a simple set of diegetic rules, genre theories or personal experiential accounts. Rather, film (and other screen-based media) theories are looking at the production and measurement of time as a part of a complex network of film production, where time factors as a human labour-fed technological product of capitalism, and film has a limited time set for its commodification period. For example, Sean Cubitt describes those films that elicit 'wonder and despair' (as in Doane's choice of death films caused both emotions for her) as 'not so much interminable' (2004: 294), but uncomfortable, non-communicative. Of the *cinéma du look* of Leos Carax (given as an example among others), Cubitt notes that it is a manipulated 'pleasure of seeing', as this cinema has 'nothing to sell, beyond the ticket that has already been sold: [it is] a postcommodity' (2004: 296). If 'we' are merely participants in the cycle of capitalist exchange, then are the filmmakers more than theorists more critical in their critique, subversion and/or delight in the connections of 'human and machine' (ibid.) that enables the creation of technology images of this system? There are, of course, exceptions.

Film theories that take the Russian school of Vertov and Eisenstein often address the perceptual awareness of the (material, technological, ideological) relationships between things generated by the use of the materials of cinematic technology. Jonathan Beller writes: 'For Vertov, film is the technology that will provide the utopian inspiration and practical means for the arrival of socialism' (2006: 37). Beller's thesis, as I examine more closely in chapter three, focuses on the ways in which a perceptual economy feeds capitalist production, but his arguments are underpinned by his advocacy of the materiality of the technological platform of the movie camera as the driver of this process. The context of this argument can be developed through Bernard Stiegler's work on cinema, as discussed in the introduction to think through the processes of image grammatisation. Stiegler's work examines the role of technology in societies driven by capitalism, and argues that technology is not a metaphor for human behaviours, but that human consciousness is but a function of technologies, where consciousness is the cinema, and time is reveled 'cinemato-graphically' (see Barker 2009; Stiegler 2011: 31).

Stiegler has published thus far three volumes (more to come) in his series on *Technics and Time* (see 1998, 2009, 2011). His thesis is that technics (forms of media technologies) are what organise and constitute human memory, and these technics are currently a 'convergence' of 'analog, digital, and soon biological syntheses' (2011: 210), along with all the technical industrial technologies that are now digital. When humans die, their genetic and individual memories die with them. While genetics may contain inherited information (although how to retrieve more than just an intuitive feeling or biological dispossession, or predilection for things in the world has yet to be determined), characteristics and individual experiences can only be 'passed on' through a tertiary form (contingent upon the society, for example a book, some music, a film, a game). Stiegler refers to tertiary form as a 'third memory', an 'epiphylogenesis, in which memory is housed outside of the body through the *organization of the inorganic*; a tool, a system of writing (or speaking), a technical trace' (2011: 206). So, if we think of film as 'the digitized temporal audiovisual object', its sound-images function as a technics of our memory, supplementing it, redirecting it, and changing it (2011: 211). The salient part of Stiegler's theory is something that filmmakers already know: 'the possible is a modality of the real', because all technosciences that organise the life and experiences of a body are outside of that body, as they are constituted through an exteriorised convergence of industrial products (see 2011: 206–10). Memory is digitally retained through a process of 'new grammatical formalizations', whereby technical means media forms (films, books, music, robots, 'nanotechnical prostheses') (2011: 210), hold and constitute memory. Stiegler thinks through the cyclical nature of image production, noting that re-production is transformative (2011: 221). He thus makes some claims for a reform of capitalism towards a more individuated society that has drawn critical attention (cf. Hansen 2004; Barker 2009; Bunyard 2012). Stiegler's contribution to film theory provides one of the stronger contemporary argu-ments on the politics of technology (for further discussion and critiques of Stiegler, see Stiegler and Derrida 2002; Roberts 2006, 2012; Crogan 2010; Kember 2011).

Stiegler's philosophical address of the ontology of technology, in terms of its medium specificity (how 'life is always cinema' [2011: 16]) has ramifications for the ways in which concepts of realism, politics, ethics and humans are understood. Other thinkers of cinema plus technology also draw from philosophy on the impact of the technological on human con-sciousness, and on human activities, including Paolo Cherchi Usai (2000, 2001), Paul Virilio (1989, 1994), Donna Haraway (1991). These theories, as they pertain to film theory, provide accounts of what Stiegler calls 'the very principle of cinema: to connect disparate elements together in a single temporal flux' (2011: 15). What is the life that cinema creates, and how does film theory account for this activity, this imagined and made new place?

This is a 'reality-question', and it appears throughout film theory as either a philosophically-posed question (cf. debates in Zizek 1992; Mullarkey 2009; Rushton 2011), or as an investigation into exteriorised industrial, cinematic products (cf. Ndalianis 2006; Rascaroli et al. 2014). It maybe posed a hang-over from the twentieth century's modernist imperative of achieving the 'new' by marking difference from previous work through overt referencing techniques, which in turn act as temporal markers (of events, situations, achievements and failures), or it may be marked by research into another kind of production. The current phase is where the processes of creation rely less on already invented paradigms and their recognisable types, but employ methods that respond to the new technological conditions – some in ways similar to modes of investigation observable in early film (actualities, or recording endurance tasks, or per-formance of routines while the camera acts as silent observer; or they do follow the logic of Stiegler's thesis by re-producing in order to individuate [2011: 221]).

Stiegler's work is also highlighted by its difference from twentieth-century theories of vision and film that pursue phenomenological accounts of the experience of technologically-organised matter. For example, when Dudley Andrew draws our attention to a phenomenology of technology, the model for this already sketched out: 'Bazin, less interested [than Sartre] in the freedom of the imagination, focuses on the power of the photograph to amplify our perception, "teaching us" what our eyes alone would not have noticed' (2010: 13). The critical question would be 'whose eyes?' and 'who is us?' in this model of thinking over the perceptual field that technology creates – which relies on the notion of a 'spectator' to drive the theorisation, rather than having an automated technological driver.

From auto to audio mediation
The technologies of film sound have received more dedicated attention than other areas of film production, perhaps because sound lends itself to abstraction more readily than the pragmatics of lighting or make up. Composer Michel Chion has argued extensively and influentially for the recognition of watching film to become known as an 'audio-viewing', in order to account for the ways in which the technologies of sound direct the viewer as auditor's attention (see Chion 2009). His logic is similar to Stiegler in that his position is also for a cognition of the autonomy of the technic. There are detailed histories of film sound that offer some critical synopsis of films, but do not offer a system for theorisation in their analyses (cf. Brophy 1998, 2004). However technical, all sound books infer the same thing: sound is a composite part of the image. Sound activates certain elements in an image. A handful of theorists have dedicated their work to film sounds. Film sound can refer to a musical score, speech, noise, screen silence and chance or found sounds recorded (cf. Attali 1985; Schaeffer 2004; Chion 2005). The acoustic experience can alter the visual image in dramatic or subtle ways, as sound appeals to a different range of sensorial experiences of the auditor. Names and faces may recede into memory, but fragments of place and situation can be readily invoked through the neurological affect of audition. Sound is thus a cause whose effect exceeds itself, as it creates an emanative property. How that is produced in film, produced for film or edited in post-production for a film – all has different effects upon the film's own immanent properties (see, for example, the range of essays on sound matters in Harper *et al.* 2006).

Conclusions – technology as prosthetic reality

Technologies are game changers. They can alter the filmic paradigm quickly, subtly, but surely. When Sadie Benning made use of the Fisher Price children's video camera in the 1990s and produced films like *Girl Power* (1992) and *Flat is Beautiful* (1995), the images she made shifted a number of significant paradigms about image quality, and matching form with content (see Marks 1998). The image, as Virilio describes, is man-made technology. For him, the technology of the image is not just something that will 'take over from immediate perception', as John Lechte argues (2012: 84). Rather, like Stiegler, Virilio argues that different visual technologies enable various images to be created, and are used in specific ways to populate the world with what Virilio describes as 'dromoscopic' concepts and objects of life; where dromoscopy refers to the speeds of mediation that create 'cinematic illusion' (see 2005: 115–6; also Beckman 2010: 107). Ultimately, Virilio argues that the image *is* the body of the world, as it functions as a continuous organiser of policies of the political affects and materials that feed the movement of capitalism, where 'we are no longer seers of our world, but already merely reviewers' (2005: 37). Arguing against Virilio's vision of technology, Douglas Kellner describes Virilio as 'one of the major critics of war, technology and vision machines' who displays 'technophobic proclivities' (1999: 104).

Critiques of the technological paradigm as a vectorial and catalytic point for the expression or imagination of the change, or 'evolution', of something point to the ways in which technology has its own problematic methodologies and ideologies. Different technological platforms arrive through different forms of political facilitation. When it comes to the philosophical framework for considering technologies such as film and media then, an essentially masculinist paradigm has provided the overarching narrative that has gendered the use and the perception of technologies of all types. The error of this paradigm lies with its application of the masculinist, and thus hierarchical, application and metaphors of technology that then re-produce the gendered structure, based upon normative sex and biological determinism.

Film technology affects the content by its technological processes. One does not precede the other, and they rarely operate singularly, but the intersections of both are what determine the style and form of film produced. The type of technological platform (as technological platform, an apparatus, a machine, or as an epistemic recording and shaping device) and structure may determine or support the content. The structure and forms of film are a part of a technologically-informed process, the details of which inform film theory. As filmmakers and theorists address, making is a process that can be pre-figured, but can also be formed through an intuitive working through technology.[9] What will produce a change in form and content are the connections between technologies used (visual, audio, intertextual), and the paradigmatic theoretical terms for these processes, as well as the production team's ethos for filmmaking. Technological impact is rendered most obviously at visual and auditory levels (of which many viewers are unaware), where technical specificities are what are determining the overall trajectory of content.

In the short history of filmmaking there have been many technological revolutions. Technology is not the same as creativity, but it will provide a medium for the capture of a moment or event that may be later deemed to be creative, innovative, original, clichéd, and so on. With each change, innovation or obsolescence, comes shifts in the film grammar, where informatics, codes, images and sounds change.

Notes

1 Holt's film *Pine Barrens* (1975) is accessible through the Electronic Arts Intermix, New York: http://www.eai.org/title.htm?id=11671 (see also her essay, 'Pine Barrens', in Holt 2011).

2 The definition of film art is reflected in the choice of film screenings. Male directors dominate; 2014's film screenings include *American Dreams (Lost and Found)* (James Benning, 1984; 55 min, 16mm-to-35mm), *Soup Can* (Robert Russett, 1967; 3 min, 16mm), *A Woman of Paris* (Charles Chaplin, 1923; 82 min, 35mm, b&w, silent), *The Battle Below* (Caroline Ceniza-Levine, 2013; ca. 14 min, digital).

3 Further discussion of these points would involve a historical address of the theories of technological agency (see Feenberg 1999: 101ff).

4 For discussion of Australian-born Hollywood director Philip Noyce's reasons to shoot this film, using the argument that the commercial success is due to the Hollywood-style use of genre-marketing tactics and the address of the media debate surrounding the politics of the film, see Collins and Davis 2004: 134–9.

5 InDigEnt was a production company for independent filmmakers that

ran from 1999–2007, founded by director Gary Winick. It produced films with a limited crew and shot on miniDV (digital video). Films from the company include *Women in Film* (Bruce Wagner, 2001), *Pieces of April* (Peter Hedges, 2003), *Personal Velocity* (Rebecca Miller, 2002), *November* (Greg Harrison, 2004). (The word 'indigent' commonly refers to an artist who is poor or needy.) Zentropa was founded in 1992 by director Lars von Trier and producer Peter Aalbæk Jensen [http://www. zentropa.dk/about/historie]. The first film was *Europa* ([also known as *Zentropa*], directed by von Trier, 1990). The company became well known after its *Dogme* 95 projects and other von Trier films, including *Dancer in the Dark* (2000), *Dogville* (2003) and *Melancholia* (2011).

6   For example, see Richard Serra's 1976 film *Railroad Turnbridge* http:// www.ubu.com/film/serra_turnbridge.html

7   See also Crawford 2009 on the period of development of Hollywood sound through the arrival of immigrants fleeing the war in Europe in the 1930s.

8   *Otaku culture* refers to the groups of people who are highly technologi- cally literate in Japanese popular culture (see Ito, Okabe, Tsuji 2012).

9   We may compare films and their theorisations here; for example, the approach taken by David Lynch in *Inland Empire* (2006; and theorised by Sinnerbrink 2011), or the non-narrative of a Len Lye film such *as Free Radicals* (discussed in Sitney 1974: 269–71), or Julie Dash's elliptical approach in *Daughters of the Dust* (and its theorisation, cf. Humm 1997: 115ff), to consider the range of synergesic and autonomous technical processes at work in film production, and as noted in film theory.

3   SPECTATORS

Marianne: You really think that's important work?
Juliane: Absolutely essential.
  – *Die Bleierne Zeit* (*The Leaden Times*, Margarethe von Trotta, 1981)

There is no film or film image without the spectator and the auditor. I see an image and I respond to it, in certain learned ways. How I see the images and the complete film is contingent upon a host of factors. Where I am seeing it is as important as what I am seeing. As Virilio, Bosak and Stiegler respectively argue, the ecology of the current militarised, hydrocarbonised landscape and its materials is the everyday spectacle through which the perceptual field of the spectator-as-participant is oriented (Virilio 1989: 25, 70; Bozak 2012: 9; Stiegler 2011: 15). This re-figured landscape, with technology-images ubiquitous to everyday life, has of course had an affect on the cultures of film viewing. To go to an artist's studio or a commercial gallery to see a film is of course different to seeing a film (or a part of it) projected on an outdoor screen, or multiple screens; is different again to film theatre viewing and mobile screen spectatorship. Anne Friedberg (1993) talked about the 'mobile spectator'; the *flaneuse* who is given a degree of freedom through different technologies (for example, the bicycle), enabling her to physically experience aspects of the world previously unknown. This *flaneuse* can take her pleasure as a fan-spectator, feeding responses and ideas back into the creator if she doesn't mind sharing her creativity, without profit (see Caslin 2007). Jonathan Beller describes this spectator in terms of their 'spectatorial labour' accounted for, borrowed against and generally corruptible as a consumer-producer (2006: 113). The spectator is the 'overwhelmed' and helpless onlooker of racist and sexist violent spectacles (see Heller-Nicholas 2011: 23), which Sarah Projansky argues is only able to 'access' different subject positions as the film allows (2001: 165). And as I have described in the previous chapter, the notion of spectator must be entirely rethought through the terms that Haraway and Stiegler have proposed, whereby humans are embodied by, or dependent upon, technologies like film for their cultural orientation and memories.

The spectator of film may be the camera, it may be the scriptwriter, it may be other bodies (animate and inanimate) on-screen and off. It may be a person, the filmmaker, who turns the camera upon themselves, as Agnès Varda does in *Les Glaneurs et la glaneuse*. It may be the cries of the women as they see the results of the colonial power holder looking over their conquested territories and people, as in *La Bataille d'Alger* (*The Battle of Algiers*, Gillo Pontocorvo, 1966) or it may be the quiet humour of the women observing their lives in *Samson & Delilah* (Warwick Thornton, 2009). The spectator may be the Yorkshire Moors in *Wuthering Heights* (Andrea Arnold, 2011), territorialising, sheltering, weathering its gritstone shoulders. The spectator may be the sharks of *The Reef* (Andrew Traucki, 2010), or the bears in Werner Herzog's *Grizzly Man* (2005), checking out their human prey, testing, eating, digesting, surviving. It may be the penguins in *Encounters at the End of the World* (Werner Herzog, 2007) ignoring the humans and participating (or not) in penguin life, or it may be the humans holding the flashlights and the crabs running away from the light in Anri Sala's *Ghostgames* (2002). The spectator may be you sitting late at night at home looking for a movie to watch via a service provider and ending up watching a late-night screening of *Marie Antoinette* (Sofia Coppola, 2006), and finding yourself singing 'Hong Kong Garden' by Siouxsie and the Banshees to the cat the next day. And so on. The list of examples is endless and conditional to the modeling the theory uses, but as the examples above show, the spectator is beholden to the spectatorial situation (as a type of spectator, within a spectacle, or as a positioned subject).

Film theory refers to issues to do with spectatorship using a variety of models, using a range of expressions and neologisms in order to describe the ways in which the film, films or the cinema have influenced the sense of a spectator. Film theorists from the earliest period described their personal experiences and motivations for cinema viewing. Siegfried Kracauer, writing an account of 1940s cinema going, describes the experience of watching a film in the movie theatre in terms of a fracturing of the corporeal senses in the face of the proliferation of images (see Hansen 2012: 268–9). The terms of immersion in images can be repeated in 2014 within enormous 3D movie theatres (such as IMAX), but commonly film spectatorship is actively done in domestically-scaled conditions. The spectator in film theory changes according to the technological platform in use. Common film theoretical agendas in spectatorship theory include issues of socially-situated viewers, audience research and identification and questions concerning the production of the image, gender role ascription, race, ethnography, sexuality, the political economy of the subject, the topic of 'subjectivity' and cinema industry spectator theories involving the study of stars, celebrities, fandom, censorship – all topics that theory describes using various modeling terms (such as otherness, identification, desire, fantasy [see Lyon 1988: 245]).[1] Often each of these topics is given a week of study in a curriculum, or a chapter in a book collection, and sometimes two or more 'themes' are placed together for study, where the identified terms of 'postcolonial', 'queer' and 'race' film theory inhabit a spectatorial 'otherness' (see Rushton and Bettinson 2010: 90). The historical terms of spectatorship are tested with new models of filmmaking, and some models are now historical. Susan Hayward identifies three phases in what she calls 'spectatorship theory' (2000: 343). Her three-phase model begins stage one at the early to mid-1970s, overlooks the contributions of the early film theorists and, as a dictionary-style entry, is limited on the detail for the developments of Metz's semiotic film theories (see Buckland 2012a: 90–2 for a summary of Metz). Hayward describes stage two as regarding post-1975 feminist film theory, and stage three as 1980s (mostly feminist) film theory (2000: 343–9). These three areas provide the basis for understanding the terminology and boundaries of mainstream film theories of spectatorship. As Hayward points out, studies of spectatorship have been enlarged by cross-media platforms such as television, where film viewer reception theories were developed in cultural and media studies.

Adding to Hayward's models, post-1980s film theories have been characterised by their attention to different kinds of signification models besides the 'identification' issues of the 1970s and 1980s. These tend to be trans- and multi-disciplinary in form, drawing upon and using language and concepts applied and developed from a number of different disciplinary fields, including architecture (see Bruno 2002), gender studies (see MacCormack 2008; Williams 2008); literary criticism, political theory, philosophy, sociology, schizoanalysis (see Buchanan and MacCormack 2008), and neurosciences (see Pisters 2011) to address and argue about questions of reality and realism, reception, representation and ethics in relation to the spectator. These can be useful, creating new connections and opening new domains for thought, or they can muddy the categories of an argument. Thinking about the spectator, the subject of the image and subjectivity as imagined on screen, the audience, and film reception, involves the writing of theory across all forms, genres of film and, as discussed in chapter two, consideration of the mode of technological mediation. The grammar of this spectatorial position switches back and forth from adjective to noun as the activity of image and its form, content, potential and real meanings are argued. Instead of just thinking about the topics or genres that theories of the spectator in and of film (which gives a somewhat distorted view), in this chapter I look at some of the ways in which film theory assigns roles to the spectator and subject of the spectator in film.

One of the core problems for spectator theory presenting as a robust and plausible theory is its type and style of approach to the question of evidence. How does the author 'know' what or to whom the 'spectator' or 'subject' of the film is, is addressing, is 'feeling', or 'reacting?' Is this a singular or plural subject, a question of 'subjectivity', and/or of spectatorial position? How to we decide what is the 'normal' or central or marginal spectator? How can one make a judgement on 'audience' reaction outside of a specific sample and situation? The voice of the film theorist can present itself as the authority, the voice of critical privilege. The analysis of the components of the film, the genre, the processes of making, distributing, marketing, the formation of ideas within individual and serial films, all come together and often hinge or are supported by this skeletal 'subject' and 'spectator' who provides the political and aesthetic flesh of the film theory's argument, and thus politics. Some film theorists have developed a specific mode of analysis based on the notion of the spectator or subject, while others implicitly assume the spectator or subject will hold the same physical and economic approximation as their own, and others deconstruct the possible positions that the film assumes to be the subject spectator.

In many respects, the subject of the spectator, subjectivity and spectatorship are at the heart of all film theories. In mapping these out, we can look at the recurring topic areas. These include ideas of (i) referentiality, (ii) experience, (iii) semiology, and (iv) technology in addressing the subject/spectator. While there are multiple modalities that theory writes around the notions of the subject, subjectivity and the spectator, these four recurrent modes act as theoretical qualifiers of these topics, whether operating as an exteriorised spectator, where 'the whole of life ... presents itself as an immense accumulation of spectacles' (Debord 1994: 12) (as in Guy Debord's 'accumulation', or a film about non-human topics, for example), or as an internalising subject (as positioned by a bio-pic, or drama that focuses on specific events or conditions, for example). Further, a separation of approaches to the subject of the spectator comes through different theoretical positions on the question of 'reality' and the spectatorial 'real', which is the topic of some debate, and not only in Lacanian philosophy of film circles (cf. Zizek 1992; Rombes 2005a; Rushton 2011). First some definitions of terms, and a few notes on the film grammar of subjectivity.

Who and what is the spectator?

Film theory assigns roles to the spectator of film. When reading film theory it is worth connecting the role with the modeling method that the theorist is employing, in order to try and discern what are the aims – and biases – of the argument. The spectator holds many functions within the theoretical model. They – or it – may be given a role that is needed within the theory to complete its ambiguities, or political or poetic intentions. The spectator may be ascribed the role of the moral police or a pleasure-seeking voyeur, or a manipulated consumer or active participant who interacts and queers the authorial image. They – or it – may be presumed by the theory to be an educated, ignorant, censored or censoring spectator and auditor. The spectator may even be excluded by the writing of the theory.

Anthropomorphising, classed, gendered and racialised hierarchies of history and cultural knowledge produce distorted and inequitable political states for and of the spectator of film as subject. Within these approaches, film production is bound by those systems of production (funding and distribution) to adhere, or to rebel. The consumer, or spectator, however, is attuned to film production in various different ways than the film itself, and theory either glosses, or attends to this point. Writing an extensive critique of the 'production of the spectator', Beller draws on Marx's language and arguments to develop a theory of 'spectatorial labour' in order to describe 'the production of image-value' wherein the spectator is a part of that mediating circuit of production of the image (2006: 113). In *Das Kapital*, Marx describes how the worker must work to produce the conditions that sustain their own life, which is given to production in the form of living capital (ie, the worker's body's duration). As Beller notes, when Marx was writing, the cinema had not yet been invented, yet the conditions of labour that the words of Marx (and Engels) articulate is that of the iniquitous distribution of the profits of labour, and so Beller reasons that Marxist theory provides an appropriate model for analysis of how spectatorial life is a component of the mediating 'worksite' (Beller 2006: 112). We can imagine the same critiques against this argument as are in place for Stiegler (as discussed in the Introduction and in chapter two); whereby the 'worker' is rendered as a gender-neutral, race-neutral, class-neutral body.

If the spectator is seen as a worker in film theory, what impact does this body have (upon the film and within the theory)? While some kinds of cinemas allow interaction (artist films in public spaces), or instances of cross media 'convergence' of post-Classical cinema (see Jenkins 2008: 103–4), most film theories deny any possibility for spectatorial intervention (aside from providing the spectatorial labouring body, and its attendant industries as Beller identifies). Steven Shaviro notes that the cinema spectator in comparison to the interactive game player has absolutely no influence over the film, and argues that 'Beller underestimates the differences between cinematic and post-cinematic media' (2010: 103). Criticisms notwithstanding, there are elements of Beller's argument that we can put to work to address theorisation of spectatorial lives, rather than 'life'. Let us start with your own spectatorial labour. This involved participation in market choice, a data processing activity whereby you code in your preferences to the system, akin to recoding the algorithm that figures your digital desktop every time you make a digital choice, or 'like' something online.

So if we begin at home. Who are the domestic spectators? What kind of film/s are you in the mood for? What kinds of market systems are you immersed in that have educated your desires for consumption? The terms of the economic production of the workplace of the contemporary spectator is described by Alexis Madrigal as necessarily occupying a different place to that of the imagined labourer out at the factory for the day (or the labour of Kracauer). Intrigued by the 'absurd' detail and breadth of genre search the consumer has access to when searching the film service provider 'Netflix' for films, Madrigal asked a question and started coding the answers. So, what to watch tonight?: 'Emotional Fight-the-System Documentaries? Period Pieces About Royalty Based on Real Life? Foreign Satanic Stories from the 1980s?', Madrigal and Ian Bogost coded a programme that would allow them to find all of the subgenres that the film service provider had stored. Madrigal records that Bogost's 'magical genre generator' came back with a staggering 76,897 unique ways to describe different types of movies. The results of this, Madrigal calls 'Netflix grammar' (2014: n.p.), to which I want to connect Beller's thesis on the requirements of spectatorial labour.

What is the 'productive value' of the spectator's 'human attention' that Beller discusses, and what sorts of film grammar has it produced? (2006: 113). I want to turn to other spectator film theory to begin to answer this and explore different spectatorship theories. These can be classified as belonging to the experiential (going to the cinema) type of spectator as well as the semiotic accounts of spectatorship (which include theories of affect, for example the pornographic text; see Linda Williams on stag films [1999: 58ff]). Mary Ann Doane argues that the spectator only exists 'as an effect of discourse' (1987: 9), and this statement points to a core concern of feminist theoretical critiques of the patriarchial hierarchies that linguisitics and materialist theories of the body model (including those that Freudian desires and drives, Lancanian mirror-stage theories have generated) – that of the linguistic construction of women as other (see also McCabe 2004: 92–5). At the discursive heart of this critique of masculinist hierarchies was the 1980s early second-wave feminist film critiques, and what became known as a voyeuristic and fetishistic 'male gaze', as identified by Laura Mulvey. This critique, while limited in its binarist theorisation of heterosexual normativity, created a new grammar for theorisation concerned with gender, race and sex role image attention and spectatorial identification. While there has been significant work done on the feminist evaluation of film texts since then (cf. Mulvey 1988; Diawara 1993; Stacey 1993; hooks 1996; Humm 1997; Williams 1999, 2008; Butler 2002; Keeling 2007; Bolton 2011; Duong 2012), the salient points of Mulvey's original manifesto published in *Screen* in 1975 continue to fracture many of the premises of narrative film theories (see the discussions around this by Rich 1998; Doane and Bergstrom 1989; Merck 1992). Mulvey's thesis identifies, as Maggie Humm outlines, the 'masculinist structures of looking' (1997: 14) that structure cinema. This thesis suggests a binarist, essentialising (for all genders) approach to image analysis. Mulvey's theory is now historical however; she offered a productive (in Beller's sense of spectatorial work), and robust critique to the gender neutral apparatus theories of the previous decade, where 'the spectator' 'can do no other than identify with the camera' (Metz 1982: 49). Where Metz proffers a theory of 'unpleasure' (1982: 6), Mulvey counters with the equally problematic 'pleasure' of viewing (for analysis of Metz, see Cartwright 2008: 29ff; Rushton 2009), and describes three different modes of looking. These theories are very much concerned with an interiorised spectator, or 'interiority', as Thomas Elsaesser and Malte Hagener (2010: 61) describe, and articulate a rather mechanised, non-imaginative version of *a spectator*. Augmenting the position Mulvey and the late 1970s structuralist theorisation (see De Bruyn 2012 for a critical appraisal from an artist's point of view of this history), came voices from queer, gay, bisexual, transsexual, indigenous, non-white and other minorities that were excluded from the 'we', the 'viewer' and the 'audience' that was identified as the all-encompassing spectator, but which position their spectatorial design as *a* specific (as opposed to an abstracted) body (see Dyer 2001; Aaron 2004; Halberstam 2011).

Counter arguments to Mulvey's class- and race-neutral spectator were provided by hooks (1996), who identified the black woman as a spectator not included in Mulvey's thesis, and further expanded the discourse. More counter arguments to Mulvey's hetero-sexed spectator by Chris Straayer set out the terms of protest against heterosexual and heteronormative assumptions that ignore the queer body. In an article written after 'Visual Pleasure', Mulvey portrayed more sex-role stereotypes with allusions to transvestism in viewer-patriarchal identification models, to which Straayer offers a firm rebuttal (1995: 46). The question for film theorists, as attended to particularly by feminist film theory, is whose body is being made as image, or is bearing the image? Who or what has constructed this spectator? And how is this spectatorial position labouring within the film text?

Deconstructed spectator

These kind of questions engage a form of discourse analysis (where a recognition of the model being written is found through intentional critical discourse [see Gee 2010: 28ff]); however, they do not direct theory to the material conditions of the specific spectatorial body. Critical of the type of generically white female spectator that Mulvey (and others) focused upon, bell hooks pointed out the authoritative exclusivity in the mainstream feminist film theory of the 1980s and 1990s (1996: 205ff) as ignorant of black women's experience; of never seeing themselves on screen except in derogatory or menial labour roles, and if framed as some desirable object of attention, it is on unequal sexual terms. hooks writes: 'more than any other, media [film] experience determines how blackness and black people are seen' (1992: 5). hooks's argument concerns *agency*, an operative word and topic that has been taken further in film theories of postcolonial and contemporary world cinemas. This agency, as defined by Stuart Hall and cited by hooks, concerns identity and its spectatorial recognition of both experience, semiotics and the self-referentiality of the spectatorial nature of film. hooks refers to films including Julie Dash's *Daughters of the Dust* (which, as we discussed in chapter two, is a film whose semiotic meanings use technology as a spectatorial device), and *The Passion of Remembrance* (Maureen Blackwood and Isaac Julien, 1986), noting their 'deconstructive filmic practice' (1996: 213). When hooks cites Hall's 'vision of a critical [spectatorial] practice', she argues with him, writing that identity is constituted 'not outside but within representation', and she invites us to see film 'not as a second-order mirror held up to reflect what already exists but a form of representation which is able to constitute us as new kinds of subjects and thereby enable who we are' (1996: 113). hooks thus takes the position that theorists might oppose in terms of the desire, or fantasy, of spectatorial identification with the film as an object (of personal and cultural desire) (cf. De Lauretis 1995: 63; Chateau 2011: 171). hooks's focus is on the agential political affects of deconstruction of the notion of a classed society.[2] Using the same language, and re-arranging its predicate words, enables hooks to reveal the Mulveyian gaze as a grammatical lexicon with no black women. hooks uses language to deconstruct the poorly applied psychoanalytic terms of the Lacanian mirror stage that enabling her to move her critique away from the terms that orthodox and classical cinema analysis uses, and re-articulate her spectatorial subjectivity within the material territory of critical counter-cinema, or a political modernism (cf. Rodowick 1994; Rushton 2011: 23–4) that recognizes her. Dash's film is not concerned with creating a 'realist' text that might counter the 'unreality' of the majority. Rather, as hooks further notes, these kind of films (*Daughters of the Dust* and *The Passion of Remembrance*) 'imagine new transgressive possibilities for the formulation of identity' [enabling] 'history as countermemory' (1996: 213). Note the word formulation, not formation. hooks is writing through the predicated noun and predicated adjective that the double formula of 'black women' inscribes to put forward an idea of potentiality that exists through the exteriorisation of the spectator that this form of semiotically-gendered film creates.

The spectatorial body as written about by hooks, and others who point out the contradictions, ambiguities and possibilities of this position that film creates, is one of semiotic, material and immaterial agency (cf. Merck 1992; Straayer 1995; Rich 1998; Porton 1999; MacCormack 2012; McGlotten and Vangundy 2013). Various theoretical positions are critiqued, using forms of a shared discourse against the monolithic textual 'spectator', as Christine Gledhill argues (1988: 64); against film theory that ignores the specificity of conditions and contexts and instead argues for a spectatorship as a form of 'countermemory', as hooks describes, or as a process of grammatisation, as Stielger contends. The question for individual theory is: what kinds of structural agency are shaping the models for specific spectators? How much part does the spectator play in the process of deconstructing the clues set up by the filmmaker? The outcomes of viewing are always variable. All we can do is explore the processes as they are created in particular places (and transnational film studies have been leading the way in terms of attention to these positions, see for example the different approaches in Marciniak *et al.* 2007). How a viewing system operates is contingent upon institutional contexts where the spectator's position is written from a particular position that privileges historical hierarchies that position a spectator according to their essentialising bodies of reference.

hooks's notion of a deconstructive cinema argues that it is productive of a counter memory for some spectators. This counter memory is one that filmmakers who narrativise history, or the vernacular, provide film theorists with much to debate, as filmmakers pose the *what if?* question. With the use of deconstructive techniques comes an ambiguity that filmmakers play on, contingent upon the film (whether it is, for example challenging, alternate or parodic of 'normative' world histories).[3] This ambiguity of 'meaning' is something that theory sets out to decode, or express.

Traumatised spectator

Describing the break of cinematic codes in relation to narrative, non-commercial documentary film, Annette Kuhn argues that the decoupling of the image with its coded 'meaning' as a deconstructive technique in filmmaking provokes 'spectators into the awareness of the actual exist-ence and effectivity of dominant codes' (1982: 160). Kuhn uses the argu-ments of Brecht and Benjamin to describe the device of constructing a 'spectator-text' relation by the images of a 'counter-cinema', which she argues are 'understood to be synonymous with deconstruction' (1982: 161). Another deconstructive positioning of the spectators of history is enacted in the films of Margarethe von Trotta. This director's controversial work has invited the attention of many film theorists, including Barbara Johnston (1976), E. Ann Kaplan (1983: 104–12) and Thomas Elsaesser (1989: 233; 2013: 139). *Die Bleierne Zeit* (also known as *Marianne and Juliane* and *The German Sisters*), is a fictionalised drama of the lives of Christiane and Gudrun Ensslin (a member of the Red Army Faction), set in Germany between 1950 and 1980. A flashback scene in the first half of the film provides some background educational context for the sisters, and their roles as participatory spectators of what Susan Linville describes as the 'frustration and disappointment' of the 1970s' promises of 'social transformation' (for the patriarchal familial unit; equal rights for all gen-ders for work, pay, reproductive rights, and childcare) (see Linville 1998: 85). The scene is in a classroom, with the camera shot taken from the back of the room, looking over the heads of the school girls. They are watching a projection of Alain Renais's film on the Nazi concentration camps, *Nuit et brouillard* (*Night and Fog*, 1955). During the footage showing the Russian liberators bulldozing hundreds of skeletal dead bodies of the inmates who perished into pits, is a point of view of the shot that makes it appear that the bodies will be pushed by the bulldozers onto the heads of the school children and bury them – along with their country's history. Reverse shots of the sisters shows them as the traumatised spectators of this event, and the film repeats the condition of survivors, observing their liberation: 'they looked on, uncomprehending'. Repeatedly through this film, argues Susan

Linville, 'certain reflexive segments of the film that foreground spectator positioning politicize spectatorship in compelling ways' (1998: 90). In her film *Hannah Arendt* (2012), von Trotta repeats this strategy of multiple, complex and often contradictory spectatorial points of view, where spectators of events (both real and narrativised by mediation; see Berkowitz 2013 for a comparative synopsis of events) are themselves then subjected to being made the objects of specular attention, by the position of the camera shot, and the film structure. Von Trotta's film deconstructs the notion of memory, through the structure of the film, and through the performance of the spectator of history (as performed by the actor Barbara Sukowa who plays both Marianne in *Die Bleierne Zeit* and Hannah in *Hannah Arendt*), whose material absoluteness forces other spectators within each film to question their memories, and the film images provoke the need to create counter and/or new cultural memories.

Arguing against the strategy of a *counter cinema* (a term described in film theory by Claire Johnston [1976]), or a grammatisation of technocultures where there is no individuated viewer, only participants, or spectatorial labourers (see Beller 2006; Steigler 2011), are film theories that propose an individual spectatorial model, one who is able to decide on her own ethical and aesthetic position. Included in this is the turn to spectatorial theories of affect (cf. Cartwright 2008; Young 2009; Boljkovac 2013), and trauma (cf. Walker 2005; Kaplan and Wang 2010; Grønstad 2011), applied to a range of subjects. If I take one recent example and situate its theory within the previous discussion, we can see where the terms of the 1970s attention to a materialist cinema, and the 1970s and 1980s attention to spectatorial roles, and invisibility of racial and gender issues have been theoretically turned.

Taking Metz's notion of 'unpleasure' to argue against the strategy of a counter cinema, Catherine Wheatley (2009), for example, develops a new spectatorial theory of unpleasurable viewing. She subscribes to an auteurist grammar to describe a spectatorial position of 'the audience', and proposes that there is an 'ethics' at stake in their viewing, examining behavioural and emotional issues such as 'guilt' in relation to the spectator (2009: 157). Following the words of director Haneke: 'art is the only thing which can console us' (cited in Wheatley 2009: 106), she describes how a counter cinema is only 'addressed to a relatively limited audience' (2009: 86) and, again citing Haneke, argues that the 'goal' of the filmmaker is 'moral reflection in and of itself, not reflection upon a set of political themes' (2009: 106) – the latter being one of the main critiques against von Trotta's films (see Linville 1998). Wheatley describes deconstruction as a 'modernist technique' (2009: 24) that is seen in the works of directors such as Michelangelo Antonioni and Chantal Akerman. Setting up a binary argument (modernist versus not modernist), Wheatley argues that the later Haneke films are not modernist in the ways that Akerman's and Antonioni's are, but instead Haneke offers a 'position of ethical spectatorship ... tailored to what the director terms 'the willing consumers of the cinema of distraction' (2009: 11). The question of who these consumers are is modified in Wheatley's later reading of Haneke's work (2013), where she posits a more specific audience. She partially reads Haneke with Kant, a philosopher concerned with morals and aesthetics, creating a dialectic proposition, given Kant's concern with peace and Haneke's obsession with violence, and Wheatley's theory has received a favourable critical response (see Chen 2009; Orr 2009).

In the case of Haneke's film *Funny Games* (to which Wheatley refers, both 1997 and 2007 versions), she argues that this film forces the viewer into making a choice about the ethics of their spectatorship of an abhorrent and violent narrative, however parodic it may be. Wheatley's theory is framed by her position on subjectivity as sovereign, asking the question: 'Why is the director doing this to me, the spectator?' (2009: 189). The 'choice' of her final 'ethical spectatorship' offers an internalisation of the spectator (in contradistinction to hooks's exteriorisation of her spectatorial subjectivity), and is a controversial position to take in terms of the director's (frequently repeated) stated wish to 'rape the viewer into autonomy' (which Wheatley cites as part of her argument; 2009: 78). Other theorists have commented upon the affects upon the viewer, and on the film form, through Haneke's excessive thematisation of violence (see T. Brown 2013). For example, Mattias Frey (2003) draws a parallel with Haneke and the 'Holocaust depiction theory' developed by Claude Lanzmann, where film deliberately does not depict violent acts on screen, but shows the conditions and the situations of the known and implicit violence (see Saxton 2008: 20, 27). Hanake in *Funny Games* explicitly and purposefully depicts violent actions; there is no direct allusion to the Holocaust, yet mindless violence evokes comparison to other fascist events. However, Frey argues that 'Haneke concentrates on the suffering of victims, rather than allowing the spectator to identify with any pseudopsychological motivation of the perpetrator; he uses a slow tempo in montage and camera to allow audience a distanced "thinking space"' (2003).

'Viewers of...'
The productive value of the spectator is discussed by theories in a number of different ways, and for different ends. The notion of an 'ethical spectatorship' is part of a concern in film theory that sits alongside a review of the inherent anthropomorphism in theoretical undertakings (cf. Minh-Ha 1991; Downing and Saxton 2009; Pick 2011; Cooper 2013; Choi and Frey 2013; Pick and Narraway 2013). In terms of a feminist film theory of spectatorship, troubled by the excessive violence toward women on screen and its consequences (see Heller-Nicholas 2011), Tania Modeleski's work (2005) points to the implicit violence towards women in Hitchcock's films, and the ways in which they lend themselves to film theory's ambiguous interpretations; for some spectators to be complicit with, and for sexist viewers to continue to be 'viewers of' as Sean Cubitt describes the audience construct (2004: 333).

Counter cinema, or deconstructive methods, whether or not achieving a shift in spectatorial positions (as accounted for in film theory), are expressed as strategies that are commonly used in experimental and artists' films, as well as mainstream cinemas. In addition to the 'realist' modes of filming that Haneke's work realises, the use of historical, found, 'amateur' and archival materials is seen as being utilised for purposes of deconstructing or interrogating the image (as noted by Connolly 2009: 115). Unintentional deconstructive practices are documented in the home spectators of found footage, and home movies (cf. Rascaroli *et al.* 2014), and these styles of filmmaking (hand-held, non-'professional') have found their way into many mainstream films (such as Haneke's *Funny Games*, *Melancholia* [Lars von Trier, 2011] and *The Bling Ring* [Sofia Coppola, 2013]), where theories of spectatorial and subject identification are drawn, using models of cognitive manipulation and affective persuasion in relation to these filmmaker's aesthetics. We might also consider the theorisation of desire, beyond Metz, Mulvey and Beller's semiotically-inscribed worker, which articulates the enjoyments of cinema despite its co-option by the global market. In her book *Cinesexuality,* using the language of Deleuze and Guattari's work post-Lacan, Patricia MacCormack describes spectatorship as an 'Inter-Kingdom Desire', where cinesexuals seek out a connection with cinema, as a potential 'distribution of intensities' that the 'plane of desire' created by film can offer (2008: 1). These intense moments, experienced, but not cognitively processed until perhaps prompted by further connectives, are experiential, but also semiotic, a-signifying and, in Guattarian terms, existential modelings.

In film theory then, we can regard subjectivity, and/or individuation, as one of the organising principles of the film work. Where subjectivity is produced as a value, then that value is the content and the technology becomes simultaneously in and of itself. Dziga Vertov's 1923 manifesto 'Kinoks: A Revolution' notes this phenomenon when it proclaims: 'I am kino-eye. I am builder. I have placed you, whom I've created today, in an extraordinary room which did not exist until just now when I also created it' (1985: 17). But Vertov (the pseudonym of director David Kaufman) is referring to his specific film oeuvre, produced within the context of post-1920s Russian revolution that aimed to connect the subjects (the daily routines of the city-living Russian people) with the frame of the kino-eye (that his cinematographer brother Mikhail Kaufman positioned in films such as *Man with the Movie Camera*, 1929). This type of subjectivity is nevertheless one that we still find in documentary styles, and in confessional modes, variously described in film theory such as 'a turn to the subject', as Michael Renov argues of 1990s documentaries (2004: xi). Investigation of the connections and affects of the spectator produced the film's material-technical processes (editing, framing, sound) is usually described in theory by their era of production, for example, of early cinema (cf. Eisenstein 1977; Gunning 1986; Schwartz 1995), which contrast with those theories of late twentieth-century technological-material and technological-philosophical concerns (cf. Cubitt 2004; Bozak 2012; W. Brown 2013), or of ethnographic performance (Rouch as shaman-trance-cameraman).

If I follow Beller's thesis a little further, the point of this home work as subject and spectator of one's own life would be in order to replenish the life of the worker-body as a living capital body, ready to face another day, at work. Is the interest in self-photography and self-film a case of the material production of a self-agency, or an affirmation of spectatorial identity (as utility or as existential worth) through a referral to the bio-political spectatorial position offered by von Trotta, or the aesthetic of Haneke's 'distracted' spectator?

For Hamid Naficy, the production of political register is to be found in screen media that depict a modal shift, or break; moments where the ethics of choice is presented. This is the subtractive movement that determines aesthetic form and the political organisation of things. Naficy refers to this moment as productive of an 'accented' cinema, which charts films where filmmakers of postcolonial, or non-Western experience chart displaced, homeless, migrants, minorities, refugees, and where a specific 'structure for feeling' (2001: 26) within a film is established by the film's techniques. It may take the form of a testimonial (see Hongisto 2012). One of the key forms within an accented cinema is the presence of an epistolarity (a writing or receiving of a written document, such a letter, or communication by telephone), which may take the form of a letter-film (such as in Akerman's *Je tu il elle*), and these forms of grammatisation complements the themes of the accented film, which are about exile, and deterritorialisation (see Naficy 2001: 10–39).[4]

Naficy argues that spectators 'like authors, are not only subjects of texts but also – Barthes to the contrary – subjects in history, negotiating for positions within psychosocial formations, producing multiple readings and multiple author and spectator effects' (2001: 34). Drawing on Naficy's description of this multiple production, Bruce Bennett and Imogen Tyler (2007) examine the politics of the border, questioning the terms by which the production researched and narrativised the bio-pic of an Afghan refugee's journey from a camp in Pakistan to England, in search of the imagined better life in the 'West', in Michael Winterbottom's *In This World* (2002). Winterbottom, as spectatorial author, ends up producing an effect that we might classify under Naficy's observation of exile as a deterritorialised life of 'confinement and security' (2001: 187ff), but which we can also observe in terms of the material ethics of the technological intervention by the camera-as-spectator.

The premise of a 'better life' is grounded in the materialist terms of the act of migration. Bennett and Tyler attend to these material facts of *In This World*, discussing the production notes, the difficulties of filming and the ramifications the film as docudrama has had on the protagonist's mediated life, post-immigration. These material aspects are foregrounded by the authors' model of theory. While it reads as largely empirical, through the use of secondary research to write a report of the pre- and post-production events of the film, the authors describe their method as the use of a 'transnational feminist critical approach to the analysis of cinema which requires a consideration of the film within various contexts' (2007: 22). This position turns out to be a neutral feminist position and an empirical review of material that is 'supplementary' to the actual film including things like production notes, interviews with the director and DVD commentaries (convergence materials), placing Bennett and Tyler as semiotic and referential spectators. This 'reception' of the work is no less subjective; this controversial film sets up the topics of the myths of the Western dream, the economics of immigration and the illegal smuggling trade (see the various subjective viewpoints on the film given by different political spectators in the *Guardian* [2003]). In addition, the film's narrative presents for the viewer a spectacle of the political, psychological, physical and economic suffering of another at a micro level. The authors piece together the spectacle for the reader – whom they named as a 'Western border tourist' (2007: 34). *In This World* is discussed for what the authors name as its 'exemplificiation' of 'Western perspectives of the border' (2007: 33), and describe it as a 'highly affecting film' that operates within a 'register of political affect', which is 'more ambiguous' than the register of 'political effect' – as it does not offer any 'solutions' or 'factual insight into the refugee crisis' of the area (2007: 22, 27). While the terms of affect are not described by the authors, their key three references throughout their essay are to Judith Butler (1993), Sara Ahmed (2000) and Hamid Naficy (2001); each of whom offer an account of the spectator through the body of themselves as authors from a lived spectatorial position. Naficy provides the conceptualisation of the affective political register that Bennett and Tyler apply, the latter using the terms *invitation, imagination, illumination, sentimentality* throughout their article, expressive of an interiorised state of the spectacle of the spectatorial labourer, exiled from his family, and now working as a dishwasher in London, although fully aware of his life as virtual, filmic spectacle. He is now absent from his birth community. Thomas Elsaesser describes this shift in the mediated spectacle, and the subject of the spectator:

> The new contract between spectator and film is no longer based solely on ocular verification, identification, voyeuristic perspectivism, and 'spectatorship' as such, but on the particular rules that obtain for and, in a sense, are the conditions for spectatorship:

the (meta-)contact established by the different interpretative communities with the films, across the rules of the game: that each
community deems relevant and by which it defines itself: its 'felicity conditions' as linguists might say. (2009: 37–8).

Definitions of degrees of the subject and produced subjectivity of various spectatorial, and/or participatory modes of viewing as engendered
through film watching and cinema-going have produced a plethora of
notions, jargon and ideas for and from the film theorist. In the introduction
to *Perverse Spectators: The Practices of Film Reception*, Janet Staiger writes
that the 'job of a reception historian is to account for events of interpretation and affective experience' (2000: 1). A neutral position is unattainable,
as there is no such thing as unmediated expression, but a separation can
be made between the problems of articulation of an argument with bias,
and the description and analysis of the 'extraordinary room' of the filmic
reality. Different types of film theory invite us to speculate on the types of
subjectivity modeled according to the normative goggles of the theorist,
for example, gendering, racialising or activating behavioural modes, and
they will style the forms of industrialisation of the subject as spectator. As
Elsaesser implies, within the rules of the game, there are many excluded
spectators in film.

The excluded spectator
Reasons for exclusion are varied. Deleuze, after Guattari, refers to the missing spectators as part of a 'minor cinema'. The absent spectator is a 'people
to come'; they are absent from viewing and from being in film because of
reasons of genocide, migration and activities of militarism (see Deleuze
1989: 221; Colman 2011: 156–8). Subject and spectatorial exclusion has had
a number of effects upon film theoretical developments, the most obvious
of which came from feminist, queer and sociological and political theorisation of the excluded spectator or subject in film. As I have discussed, bell
hooks pointed out the exclusion in Mulvey's thesis on 'the gaze' as a primary
method of construction of meaning and, thus spectatorial identity. hooks
argues that 'an oppositional gaze' is developed to the dominant order, as
identified by mainstream (feminist) film theory (hooks 1996: 208).

But in hooks's formulation of an ultimately more empowering sense
of spectatorial agency, her theory provides a way of thinking about the

impasses that racialised hierarchies present. Mulvey's theory named a set of issues that hooks was then able to more clearly articulate through a deconstructive method of writing, naming the black female spectator. In her discussion of subjectivity and historical systems in the film *Orlando* (Sally Potter, 1992), Maggie Humm cites a famous phrase from Virginia Woolf's source novel, *Orlando*, which notes that: 'It is these pauses that are our undoing. It is then that sedition enters the fortress and our troops rise in insurrection' (see Humm 1997: 171). Jacques Rancière argues: 'Emancipation begins when we challenge the opposition between viewing and acting; when we understand that the self-evident facts that structure the relations between saying, seeing and doing themselves belong to the structure of domination and subjection' (2009: 13). The term that Rancière uses for the excluded spectator is 'emancipated'; by which he means that the spectator who is not versed in 'knowledge' of the discipline, but is able to reorder and interpret what she has seen, comparable to her own experiences. In addition, Rancière argues: 'What the spectator *must* see is what the director *makes her see*' (2009: 14; emphasis in original). This position may well be challenged by feminist film theorists, whose work points to the specifics of spectatorial exclusion, as well as those based on economic and social circumstances, such as Rancière mentions (but provides male gender case studies by way of his examples).

The spectator is *part of* the technology that creates the film *spectacle*. In addition to film theory's challenge to the spectator-auditor-participant, within films, spectators are set up as functions of the crafted film. The filmic 'truth' relies entirely on the spectator's ability, and willingness, to 'believe' in the world in front of them, for its duration, and in its affective reach of sensorial and cognitive, and intuited, resonances. Different film theorists do of course approach this spectator as willing or unwilling, complicit, or ignorant, cineliterate, or immature, and provide for them different schema, diagrams, models and measures, with which to 'access' all of the action, forms and 'meanings' of that imbrication, or enfolding of the spectatorial self into the technologically-crafted film world. Accounts that describe this type of shared discourse often refer to the material-technological-economic model of spectatorship, for example Raymond Bellour (2012) describing the change in the film medium, effected by the spectator, in terms of the difference of watching a film in a cinema theatre to watching that same film on a hand-held screen.

The connection to technology by theory is varied by a number of spectatorial and other factors concerning subjectivity and its performance. Does the theory discuss or address any complicity or critical awareness of connections of the techno-filmic-spectatorial body concerning roles allocated by economic or gendered factors? Does it address the connections produced or created? For example, the embodied movement digitally recorded by a *gopro* camera strapped to the body in action, or the limited time for a scene to be shot in front of an analog film strip of finite length. In contrast to the second wave feminist, postcolonial and/or national cinema theorisation that seeks to account for the specific body of the spectator of films (cf. Chaudhuri 2005; Cua Lim 2009), film theories do argue for the spectatorial position of a shared experience of viewing, sometimes with a qualifying body, but often from a gender or body neutral position (cf. Debord 1994; Cherchi Usai 2001; Chateau 2011). In the conceptualisation of the experience of 'going to the movies', 'the film experience'; the description of the film image as a referential cultural and political marker by its gender, sex, race, spiritual and labour roles, as a semiotic indicator and manipulator of public knowledge and political ideas, film theory and philosophies of film are divided in their positions and geographically and temporally contingent opinions.

Each positioning of the spectator in theory impacts upon the formal language of film theory, on the construction of different modes of cinematographically produced 'reality', and on the ways in which that the spectator carries that filmic impact into other arenas of life. *It was just like a film* becomes *we should film this*, or *filming makes it strange/empowering*, or *that film changed the way I think about x, or that film makes me think about memory/reality/geology/and so on.* What film theory has to write in response to the image in relation to the spectator, spectatorship and the subjects ascribed therein involve values concerning subjectivity – as raced, gendered and classed by their actions, activated and aesthetic preferences, and consideration (or not) of the political and economic systems that affect these positions.

In the conceptualisation of the experience of these film worlds and their created film images, film theory and philosophies of film will ascribe a certain kind of spectator to the film world. Film theory gives a name to the body implicated by the film image. Or the theory ignores that body, and assumes a universal body, one that generally turns out to be the normative body of the historical time of writing, which may or may not affect future theorists to engage an anachronistic argument, or a gender/ethnic/politically motivated gender anachronistic writing. In addition, a branch of film theory deals with the issue of perverse spectatorship, in terms of a cultural but also political transformation of the public sphere (cf. Staiger 2000: 32; Halberstam 2011). The spectator may be one that still watches a film on a screen, alone, in her darkened room or theatre, but the terms of her watching have been mediated by other modes of spectatorial knowledge and access, contingent upon geographic, economic, technological, gender based and cultural accesses to her public sphere.

Conclusions: There is no I in spectator, but there is a body – human and non-human
Francesco Casetti writes that the consideration of the cinema as 'a locus of experience' is 'necessary' for three reasons: 'reception ... representation and production'. Casetti argues that there is a missing coda to these 'three pillars' of film theory, stating that: 'A spectator does not find herself "receiving" a film: she finds herself "living" it' (2011: 53).

In addition to this embodied life of the spectatorial labourer, or spectator as aesthete, we must note that the centrality of the spectatorial position in film theory has been out of synch with other humanities' theoretical critique and rejection of the centrality of the human subject of theory. Spectatorship theory in film studies throughout the first hundred years of its discipline was dominated by self-referential and human-experiential discussion of the spectator of film.

Filmmaking is a human activity, but its subjects are frequently not human, and as many theorists argue, the many autonomous aspects of film (pre- and post-production) mean that they ascribe an ontological status to film; film as another being, and as not human, but creative of film in the sense that humans ascribe 'creativity'. In the late 1990s, a critique of the implicit anthropocentrism of film theorisation was driven by second-wave feminist theory (see Humm 1997). Theories from this decade are marked by their attention to the role of the spectator given the changes in the economic, architectural and technological site of the cinema auditorium. Given the technological, machinic platform of the camera which records another viewpoint of all matter in the world, seen and unseen, filmmaking practice does tend to split itself into the natural world, non-human and object-oriented films and those that are human-centred (which may also engage in the non-human worlds). Donna Haraway, Paolo Cherchi Usai, Sean Cubitt, Thomas Elsaesser, Patricia MacCormack, amongst others have debated the changes in the subject, audience, participant and/or cinematic spectator, due to the changes in technology over time. Theories involving the spectator produced more ideas and made more connections about how film might influences, cognitively determine, or affect the viewer, as a consumer or participant of certain roles. Film theory in the 2010s posits its critical demands in terms of a non-human audience (cf. MacCormack 2013; Pick and Narraway 2013; Tormey 2013).

The question of viewing, of spectatorship, and of the spectator of and in film theory is a complex one. There is no singular theory of the spectator, and each theorist will devise their theory according to quite different methodologies, conceived through a mix of interdisciplinary approaches. Yet even when film theory does not explicitly address the question of spectatorship, this activity, as an active construction and participation in the filmic world is implicitly driving the construction of the theory.

Some are born to sweet delight.[5]

Notes

1   The 'subject' in film theory holds a range of positions. Existing film
     theory divides them into the following categories and associated
     words, concepts and genres:
     Anthropocentric
     Ethnographic
     Experiential [including apparatus, cinephilic, cognitive]
     Frankfurt School critiques [perceptual, publics, scopophilic,
         voyeuristic]
     Ethical [tragic, documentary]
     Gendered [including desire, sexed, sutured]
     Vernacular
     Sensorial [including affective, auditory, desiring, haptic,
         mnemonic, sexual]
     Historically subjective
     Informational [pedagogic]
     Imaginary [including symbolic, fetishistic, mnemonic, fantasy,

phantasy]

Ludic [animated, serialised]

Materialistic [fetishistic, action, object-subject]

Neurological [including mnemonic, counter memory]

Political [ideological, modernism]

Psychoanalytic [including apparatus, desiring, fetishising, narcissistic, schizoanalytic]

Semiotic [cognitive, index, indexical, linguistic, comedic, romantic]

Technical [including apparatus, narcissism, sound]

2   Deconstruction is a term that has had a variable historical use in film theory. A method proposed by Derrida, its intention was to find a way out of the binary structures that structuralist politics and thinking maintained, by engaging in a very close analysis of the text, paying particular attention to its language, and contradictions (see Derrida 1976, 1978; Malabou 2010). Mark Hansen (2004) has described how Stiegler's project itself deconstructs Derridian grammatology with the concept of grammatisation, enabling a new use of the methodology of deconstruction to engage the materiality of technocultures.

3   A selection of films that engage in this sense of counter or deconstruction or parody includes: *Fuses* (Carolee Schneemann, 1967); *Belle de Jour* (Luis Buñuel, 1967); *Planet of the Apes* (Franklin J. Schaffner, 1968); *Theorem* (Pier Paolo Pasolini, 1968); *Aquirre, Wrath of God* (Werner Herzog, 1972); *Pepi, Luci, Bom, and Other Girls on the Heap* (Pedro Almodovar, 1980); *The Life and Times of Rosie the Riveter* (Connie Fields, 1980); *A Question of Silence* (Marleen Gorris, 1982); *Videodrome* (David Cronenberg, 1983); *Born in Flames* (Lizzie Borden, 1983); *Night Cries: A Rural Tragedy* (Tracey Moffatt, 1989); *Raise the Red Lantern* (Zhang Yimou, 1991); *Rambling Rose* (Martha Coolidge, 1991); *Orlando* (Sally Potter, 1992); *Go Fish* (Rose Troche, 1994); *Underground* (Emir Kusturica, 1995); *Dark City* (Alex Proyas, 1997); *Jackie Brown* (Quentin Tarantino, 1997); *Velvet Goldmine* (Todd Haynes, 1998); *The Virgin Suicides* (Sofia Coppola, 1999); *Otto; or Up with Dead People* (Bruce LaBruce, 2008).

4   For a discussion of deterritorialisation see Deleuze and Guattari 1987: 142–5; to see the concept applied in film analysis see Colman 2011: 149–50.

5   Nobody (Gary Farmer) reciting the words of William Blake, to William
    Blake (Johnny Depp), in *Dead Man* (Jim Jarmusch, 1995). Nobody acts
    as an internal and external spectator-narrator of the multiple contexts
    of this film (cf. analysis of this film in Nieland 2001; Colman 2009b).

CONCLUSIONS: FILM THEORY AS PRACTICE

The only possible conclusion is that an enormous amount of work
still remains to be done.
  – Peter Wollen, *Signs and Meaning in the Cinema* (1969: 156).

The question most often asked about films seems straightforward: *What is
the film about?* Yet to answer is not so simple, without engaging the most
simplistic of value judgments: 'I liked it', or 'it was good', or 'I didn't like it
', or 'it was bad'. Such answers are pure judgements based on subjective
aesthetic criteria. While aesthetic preferences (which convey the contextual
spectrum of value systems of political, moral, religious, economic, sexual,
spiritual persuasion) form a part of the critical field, different choices for a
modeling method will inevitably privilege one epistemic mode of thinking
over another.

The film ends and the work of film theory begins. In Margarethe von
Trotta's *Die Bleierne Zeit,* a confrontational scene between the two sisters
plays out with each questioning the value of the other's work. The script
embraces the materiality of their language and of their technological
mediation explicitly; through institutions of religion, family, education and
the law, and through the media of film, journalism and their predicated
active bodies. Each invests time, labour and ultimately their entire life in
commitment to their beliefs, in theory parallel, in practice oppositional.
There is always a separation between theory and practice, even when

one's practice is the craft of writing, as the action of writing proceeds like every practice, perhaps within a model, plan or schema, but the action, however well designed, or not, will precede the intention. While the filmic sound-image continues to play within the minds of the beholders, film theory's challenge is to not just respond to the film (this is the task of the film review), but to begin to direct readers toward a specific theoretical framework. The film theorist is a director of not just the film images, but of the potential of those images to infer and connect, of the film to be positioned in or outside of other films and images; of the cinema to be productive of certain kinds of thinking and of seeing the world and worlds of the imagination.

The work of the film theorist is to work with what exists, and what is imagined. One must choose which creative spectrum to work with. In this short book, I have attempted to provide an overview of three of the essential elements for the practice of film theorisation: first, a consideration of what kind of model of theory is being applied (as an epistemic method); second, a reminder to look at the technological platform being used to make the object of theory; and third, critical questions regarding what kind of cinematic spectatorship is in operation in theorisation.

Film theory has a short hundred-plus year history that provides some wonderful and traumatic images on the history of the twentieth century through which it developed, and images of alternative and fantastical worlds that counter or parallel that history. In its contemporaneous writing there are specific authors of this film theory; the film theorists, collectively they have produced this grammar and its rules. Its collective history has now produced an array of voices and theories. Online resources continue to swell the informational pool. Film theory concepts attest to the often passionate debates about how to articulate the agency and affects of the cinematic. Film theory uses and massages words into forms that place disparate technologies, materials, ideas and life onto a platform for examination, valuation and sometimes appreciation.

Reading through a selection of the past century's film theories, I am struck by a recurring theme. This is where theory connects the technical possibilities of the cinema with the spectator, and the question of 'reality' comes to figure as a thematic question; as a 'problem' or 'puzzle' to be solved, understood, explicated. Underlying the myriad of modeling theories that film theory applies, the question of reality is something of an obsession. In broad groups there a number of ways that the question of realism has been approached in screen theory. First, are the socially active realist models engaged with political intent (Eisenstein and the Russian formalists, the Italian neo-realists, documentaries of John Harmondsworth, Agnès Varda, Connie Field, Michael Moore, Morgan Spurlock). Second, there are those interested in the technical achievement of film that enabled detailing and recording of the vernacular, the scientific, and the creation of diverse forms of film genres and narratives (Len Lye's materialist film, *Free Radicals*; Sadie Benning's use of new technologies in *Girl Power*; the magic realism of *El laberinto del fauno* [*Pan's Labyrinth*, Guillermo de Toro, 2006]) and different film theoretical paradigms (Kracauer's *materialism*, Keaton's comedies, De Lauretis's *Technologies of Gender*, Stiegler's *grammatisation*). Third, there are the approaches that critically questioned the preceding two modes, and looked to account for the nature of perception itself; through investigation into the movements of spectatorial positioning in temporal and spatialised terms (we see this evidence in the work of specific film groups, and/or individuals, and film projects, such as *Sud sanaeha* [*Blissfully Yours*, Apichatpong Weerasethakul, 2002]). Theorists are also divided into different polemical camps in terms of the interest in various accounts of reality. The question of the semiotic and/or materialist coded reality and/of realism provides the sub-context for my discussion on modeling methodologies of film theory. Those histories need to be untangled further to discern their coded agendas for the kinds of products they were interested in promoting.

As media networks rapidly and intensively increase the circulation of digitised life-images, and the technologies of film shift the traditional disciplinary understanding of that image, necessarily, the reception, theory and modeling of film has also changed. The terms of analysis of the images of film worlds seek to articulate positions on the status of the film image, variously as affective, canonic, ideological, indexical, imaginative, immaterial, experiential, locational, national, neurological, perceptual, political, as readymade, as sensorially, materially and epistemologically constituted. These various positions are articulated in relation to the media producer, film maker, theorist or philosopher as a spectator, participant or producer in and of the film world, by which they position themselves and/or the film world as a constituted, dynamic, incomplete, mediating or incomprehensible 'reality.'

This reality, for film theory, is something that is produced and circu-lated by the film image. Analyses concerning the reality as produced by film worlds range according to the modes of applied methodology used; from the anxiety concerning the technologically-driven changes in image production that occurred between analog and digital in the 1990s (as Rodowick 2007 describes these in terms of the 'virtual life' of film), to the recognisable lines of post-Platonic analytic investigations (see Carroll 1988a; Casetti 1999) or post-Bergsonian (see Munsterberg 1970; Deleuze 1986, 1989; Martin-Jones 2011; Pisters 2012) or post-Frankfurt (see Hansen 2012), post-Kantian (see Beller, Stiegler) reflections on film worlds.

The spectator-participants of film worlds are, variously, bound by their community, or are cast as a global citizen, sometimes an abstract ideal, sometimes as a function of the technology of the cinema, sometimes as subject of film, sometimes a mimetic function of the author's own body and experience. As standalone concepts, these theories of spectator, subject and reception are bound by their anthropogenic limits, authorial privileges, applied disciplinary jargon and the parochial and historically bounded fields of film theory. The historical territory that produced the film theory – its temporal, geographical, political and psychological milieu – directs the shape of its model of the conditions and situation on screen. The territory of a produced subjectivity is productive of the analysis or use of a concept or notion. As with all notions in theory, the differences in time, place, gender politics and technological shifts make some ideas not transferable, although as materially produced ideas; arising from the agential (cognitively and technologically) formed materiality of film work, then the subjective reception holds some common grounds. Visual cogni-tion – including its histories – is determined by the contemporary moment of our audio visual-cultural landscape. We can only perceive of the past and the future through the lens of now; the reader's embodied, lived dura-tion. However, the paradigm shift from film to moving image as an object of study had taken hold. The archival emphases on materiality and media archaeology currently drives this change. We understand that the indus-trial machinery of image production today includes the social (aspects of labour, art forms), the technological (not only the terms of data recoding and storage as either analog or digital, but also the political contexts of production of technology, through specific territories of gender and other economically driven, and culturally specific forms of hierarchical power institutions), and the historical cultures of film (histories, epistemologies). To articulate a texts' cognitive interests, ideological premises, aesthetic and thus political position, is to become aware of the driving forces/obsessions/passions behind a film theoretical text's narrative, again issues that are historically materially and politically contingent.

Film theory is distinct from the writing of the film archivist, film actor, film curator, film director, film distributor, film producer, film publicist, film critic, film historian, film technician, scriptwriter, photographer, blogger, tweeter, and so on. While drawing from all of these professions' writing modes, film theory creates a writing form that places the disparate media of commentaries of technologies and materials on a similar plane in order to interpret and measure their value against a range of other positions. The results are nearly always a qualitative account of an aspect that the film or its content or technical aspect enlivens in the writer. This is not an objective medium, despite protestations from those professing that they are using a 'scientific' methodology in order to explicate the filmic 'essence'.

Canonic film theories have moved 'us' through the twentieth-century notions of being an active participant, trying to piece together the ellipses produced by the sparse inter-titles of silent film, to the passive audience of propaganda nationalist newsreel of global wars, back to the participant as active consumer of entertainment industries. Yet 'we' also know that this three-point summary of the first century of cinema is partially misrepresentative of individual and whole community's experiences and understanding of the *cinécriture* of specific directors. Film theory is, more often than not, the film theorist themselves as spectator, whose memories and special political roles are produced through virtual images, the imaged territory, or the bodies of the actors of film, mediating the image through a perpetual 'liveness' (see Mazumdar 2012).

The political positions of the practitioners have also meant the continued sidelining of certain theorists' work, in blanket rejections of positions seen as 'too political' (as was the case with Pasolini), and as continues today in blind review practices of academic work. However, what needs to be detailed are some of the philosophical host positions of such political statements – not so much tied to Plato, Aristotle or Kant, but to other politically determining names: Papandreou, Berlusconi, Cameron, Merkel, Putin; the political controllers of the era of the production and destruction of cultures that make and use images. Models that methods for analysis of screen modes use are engaged through institutional structures that will validate, support, or reject and dismiss. It is in local and global political trends for governmental policy (for humanities' research funding, for example) and institutional management's economically-oriented philosophy that the directing of the type of forms that critical theorists are encouraged to conform to, or can take. The question for a film theorist begins with 'how does this work' but ends with (and I think must be the place in which film theory is situated) 'who is the host of this work?' and 'for which audience?' How does the image emerge? By what means do I, as a viewer of this image, synthesise what I see and comprehend, and am affected by? What have different forms of cinematic materiality facilitated? What have different materialist media convergences created?

Film theory describes the filmic text as a construction of many different discourses that enter the film at the site of its production and, after, its distribution. However, film theory is about the questioning of beliefs, and as such it presents an epistemologically critical materialist grammar of film, film images and the industry of cinema. These beliefs are historically determined by technology and by knowledge systems, which are dynamic. As Jean-Claude Carrière writes of film language: 'No manual of film grammar– aesthetic, practical, commercial – survives longer than ten years. Everything constantly takes itself apart and reassembles itself' (1994: 26).

Writing this book has been a difficult task, primarily for the reason that Carrière notes; film theory is a dynamic medium. In a constant state of change, film theory is responsive to its contemporaneous contexts, engaged with the language of its productive era, the recognition of which shifts as the sciences, technologies and the politics that drive and govern societies redirect attention and affect creative practices that are attentive to and governed by a range of institutional, economic and personal factors. Yet the time of change is not always rapid – it may take centuries before potentials of the cinematograph are realised, but to what political and thus ecological ends we can only but speculate. Although I have been teaching film theory at universities since the early 1990s, and have worked closely with artist and student filmmakers for just as long on the processes of articulation of the moving sound-image, I find re-reading each of the published texts at different times and different places both exciting and frustrating, as they are in constant dialogue with new and changed developments and directions. My models for 'good theory' also shift and change as I forget what I have learned and some of what I have seen, and then find new things, new images, and find myself redirected to different theoretical paradigms. Thus the words written by Teresa De Lauretis in 1984 can be as salient as those that Germaine Dulac penned in 1925. The advocacy of certain film theses can present useful knowledge on filmmaking processes, but when framed in problematic terms (for example as sexist, or racist, or even as gender or generationally blind) then grammars of exclusion in operation require naming. If, as Pasolini writes, 'reality is, in the final analysis, nothing more than cinema in nature' (2005: 198), then the spectator is required by that cinematic reality to develop a language that will account for what the cinema expresses, in non-representational terms, critique what 'nature' is representative of, and further, as Deleuze writes, 'to make visible, relationships of time which cannot be seen in the represented object and do not allow themselves to be reduced to the present' (1989: xii). Film theory often describes the 'how it works' in terms of the technics of film editing, cinematography and production, but that discussion may be at the expense of a consideration of what that construction is depicting about the political and aesthetic situation of a subject.

Expanding research through the development of different arguments where categorically possible by plugging ideas to different theoretical modes enables new theories to begin to formulate. The trick is to renew one's own perceptual and polemic capacities by connecting films with texts through one's own words and responses. I am aware of all that is not included in here, or what has been glanced over for the sake of word economy. All I can do is indicate the paradigms that I think may be useful for future work in this teenage discipline.

SELECT BIBLIOGRAPHY

Aaron, M. (ed.) (2004) *New Queer Cinema: A Critical Reader*. New Brunswick, NJ: Rutgers University Press.

Abel, R. (ed.) (1988) *French Film Theory and Criticism 1907–1939: A History/ Anthology, volume one 1907–1929*. Princeton, NJ: Princeton University Press.

Adorno, T. and H. Eisler (1994 [1947]) *Composing for the Films*. London: Althone.

Ahmed, S. (2000) *Strange Encounters: Embodied Others in Post-Coloniality*. London and New York: Routledge.

Aitken, I. (2002) *European Film Theory and Cinema: A Critical Introduction*. Bloomington, IN: Indiana University Press.

Alaimo, S. and S. Hekman (eds) (2008) *Material Feminisms*. Bloomington, IN: Indiana University Press.

Althusser, L. (1971) *Lenin and Philosophy and other Essays*, trans. B. Brewster. New York: Monthly Review Press.

Altman, R. (2007) *Silent Film Sound*. New York: Columbia University Press.

Amago, S. (2010) 'Ethics, Aesthetics, and the Future in Alfonso Cuarón's *Children of Men*', in *Discourse*, 32, 2, 212–35.

Andrew, D. (1976) *The Major Film Theories*. New York: Oxford University Press.

___ (1984) *Concepts in Film Theory*. Oxford: Oxford University Press.

___ (2006) 'An Atlas of World Cinema', in S. Dennison and S. H. Lim (eds) *Remapping World Cinema: Identity, Culture and Politics in Film*. London and New York: Wallflower Press, 19–29.

___ (2010) *What Cinema Is!* Oxford: Wiley-Blackwell.

Andrews, D. (2013) *Theorizing Art Cinemas: Foreign, Cult, Avant-Garde, and Beyond*. Austin, TX: University of Texas Press.

Anthology Film Archives (2014) [Online: http://anthologyfilmarchives.org/about/about]

Appadurai, A. (1996) *Modernity at Large: Cultural Dimensions of Globalization*. Minneapolis. MS: University of Minnesota Press.

Armes, R. (1987) *Third World Filmmaking and the West*. Berkeley, CA: University of California Press.

Arnheim, R. (1957) *Film as Art*. Berkeley, CA: University of California Press.

Attali, J. (1985) *Noise: The Political Economy of Music*, trans. B. Massumi. Manchester: Manchester University Press.

Balázs, B. (1970 [1952]) *Theory of the Film: Character and Growth of a New Art*, trans. Edith Bone. New York: Dover Publications.

___ (2010) *Béla Balázs: Early Film Theory – Visible Man and The Spirit of Film*, ed. E. Carter, trans. R. Livingstone. Oxford: Berghahn.

Balibar, E. (1991) 'Racism and Nationalism', in E. Balibar and I. Wallerstein (eds) *Race, Nation, Class: Ambiguous Identities*. London and New York: Verso, 37–67.

Balio, T. (2013) *Hollywood in the New Millennium*. London: British Film Institute/Palgrave Macmillan.

Ball, S. (2011) 'Conditions of Music: Contemporary Audio-Visual Spatial Performance Practice', in A. L. Rees, D. White, S. Ball and D. Curtis (eds) *Expanded Cinema: Art, Performance, Film*. London: Tate, 267–75.

Barad. K (2007) *Meeting the Universe Halfway: Quantum Physics and the Entanglement of Matter and Meaning*. Durham, NC: Duke University Press.

Barker, S. (2009) 'Transformation as an Ontological Imperative: The [Human] Future According to Bernard Stiegler', in *Transformations*, 17, special issue on Bernard Stiegler and the Question of Technics [Online: http://www.transformationsjournal.org/journal/issue_17/article_01.shtml]

Barthes, R. (1976 [1973]) *The Pleasure of the Text*. trans. R. Miller. New York: Hill and Wang.

___ (1990a [1967]) *The Fashion System*, trans. M. Ward and R. Howard. Berkeley, CA: University of California Press.

___(1990b [1970]) *S/Z: An Essay*, trans. R. Miller and R. Howard. New York: Hill and Wang.

Baudrillard, J. (1996 [1968]) *The System of Objects*, trans. James Benedict. London: Verso.

Baudry, J.-L. (1986 [1970]) 'Ideological Effects of the Basic Cinematographic Apparatus', in P. Rosen (ed.) *Narrative, Apparatus, Ideology*. New York: Columbia University Press, 281–98.

Bazin, A. (1967 [1958–9]) *What is Cinema? Vol. 1*, ed. and trans. H. Gray. Berkeley, CA: University of California.

___ (1971 [1961–2]) *What is Cinema? Vol. 2*, ed. and trans. H. Gray. Berkeley, CA: University of California.

___ (2008 [1957]) '*De la Politique des Auteurs*', in B. K. Grant (ed.) *Auteurs and Authorship: A Film Reader*. Oxford: Blackwell, 19–28.

Beckman, K. (2010) *Crash: Cinema and the Politics of Speed and Stasis*. Durham, NC: Duke University Press.

Bell, V. (2007) *The Challenge of Ethics: Politics and Feminist Theory*. Oxford: Berg.

Beller, J. (2006) *The Cinematic Mode of Production: Attention Economy and the Society of the Spectacle*. Hanover, NE: University of New England Press.

___ (2013) 'Digitality and the Media of Dispossession', in T. Scholz (ed.) *Digital Labor: The Internet as Playground and Factory*. New York: Routledge, 165–86.

Bellour, R. (2000) *The Analysis of Film*, ed. C. Penley. Bloomington, IN: Indiana University Press.

___ (2012) 'The Film Spectator: A Special Memory', trans. A. Martin, in G. Koch, V. Pantenburg and S. Rothöhler (eds) *Screen Dynamics: Mapping the Borders of Cinema*. Vienna: Filmmuseum, 9–21.

Belsey, C. (2002 [1980]) *Critical Practice*. London: Routledge.

Benjamin, B. (2013) 'Emmanuel Lubezki, ASC, AMC and his collaborators detail their work on *Gravity*, a technically ambitious drama set in outer space', in *The American Society of Photographers*, November [Online: http://www.theasc.com/ac_magazine/November2013/Gravity/page1.php]

Benjamin, W. (1999 [1935]) 'The Work of Art in the Age of Mechanical Reproduction', in L. Braudy and M. Cohen (eds) *Film Theory and Criticism: Introductory Readings*. New York and Oxford: Oxford University Press, 731–51.

Bennett, J. (2010) *Vibrant Matter: A Political Ecology of Things*. Durham,

NC: Duke University Press.

Bennett, B. and I. Tyler (2007) 'Screening Unlivable Lives', in K. Marciniak, A. Imre and A. O'Healy (eds) *Transnational Feminism in Film and Media*. Basingstoke: Palgrave Macmillan, 21–36.

Bennett, B., M. Furstenau and A. MacKenzie (eds) (2008) *Cinema and Technology: Cultures, Theories, Practices*. Basingstoke: Palgrave Macmillan.

Berkowitz, R. (2013) 'Lonely Thinking: Hannah Arendt on Film' in *The Paris Review*, May 30 [Online: http://www.theparisreview.org/blog/2013/05/30/lonely-thinking-hannah-arendt-on-film/]

Bhabha, H. (1983) 'The Other Question: the Stereotype and Colonial Discourse', in *Screen*, 24, 6, 18–36.

Blair, H. (2001) '"You're Only as Good as Your Last Job": The Labour Process and Labour Market in the British Film Industry', in *Work, Employment & Society*, March, 149–69 [Online: http://wes.sagepub.com/content/15/1/149.short]

Blassnigg, M. (2009) *Time, Memory, Consciousness and the Cinema Experience*. Amsterdam and New York: Rodopi.

Block, A. B. (2010) *George Lucas's Blockbusting: A Decade-by-Decade Survey of Timeless Movies Including Untold Secrets of Their Financial and Cultural Success*. New York: HarperCollins.

Bobo, J. (1995) 'Daughters of the Dust', in *Black Women as Cultural Readers*. New York: Columbia University Press, 133–66.

Bogue, R. (2011) 'Giles Deleuze', in P. Livingston and C. Plantinga (eds) *The Routledge Companion to Philosophy and Film*. London and New York: Routledge, 368–77.

Boljkovac, N. (2013) *Untimely Affects: Gilles Deleuze and an Ethics of Cinema*. Edinburgh: Edinburgh University Press.

Bolter, D. J. and R. Grusin (2000) *Remediation*. Cambridge, MA: MIT Press.

Bolton, L. (2011) *Film and Female Consciousness: Irigaray, Cinema and Thinking Women*. Basingstoke: Palgrave Macmillan.

Bonitzer, P. (1986 [1975–76]) 'The Silences of the Voice (a *propos* of *Mai 68* by Gudie Lawaetz)', trans. P. Rosen and M. Butzel, in P. Rosen (ed.) *Narrative, Apparatus, Ideology*. New York: Columbia University Press, 319–34.

Bordwell, D. (1972) 'The Idea of Montage in Soviet Art and Film', in *Cinema Journal*, 11, 2, 9–17 [Online: http://www.jstor.org/stable/1225046]

___ (1985) *Narration in the Fiction Film*. Madison, WS: University of Wisconsin Press.

___ (2002) 'Intensified Continuity: Visual Style in Contemporary American Film', in *Film Quarterly*, 55, 3, 16–28 [Online: http://www.jstor.org/stable/1213701]

___ (2012) *Pandora's Digital Box: Films, Files, and the Future of Movies*. Ebook: http://www.davidbordwell.net/books/pandora.php

Bordwell, D. and N. Carroll (eds) (1996) *Post-Theory: Reconstructing Film Studies*. Madison, WS: University of Wisconsin Press.

Bordwell, D. and K. Thompson (2012) *Film Art: An Introduction* (tenth edition). New York: McGraw-Hill.

Bozak, N. (2012) *The Cinematic Footprint: Lights, Camera, Natural Resources*. New Brunswick, NJ: Rutgers University Press.

Bresson, R. (1986 [1975]) *Notes on the Cinematographer*, trans. J. Griffin. London: Quartet Encounters.

Brevik-Zender, H. (2011) 'Let Them Wear Manolos: Fashion, Walter Benjamin, and Sofia Coppola's *Marie Antoinette*', in *Camera Obscura*, 26, 1–33 [Online: http://cameraobscura.dukejournals.org/content/26/3_78/1. abstract]

Brophy, P. (ed.) (1998) *Cinesonic: The World of Sound in Film*. Sydney: AFTRS.

___ (ed.) (1999) *Cinesonic: Cinema and the Sound of Music*. Sydney: AFTRS.

___ (ed.) (2002) *Cinesonic: Experiencing the Soundtrack*. Sydney: AFTRS.

___ (2004) *100 Modern Soundtracks*. London: British Film Institute.

Brown, T. (2013) *Breaking the Fourth Wall: Direct Address in the Cinema*. Edinburgh: Edinburgh University Press.

Brown, W. (2013) *Supercinema: Film-Philosophy for the Digital Age*. London and New York: Berghahn.

Brown, D. and T. Krzywinska (2009) 'Movie-games and game-movies: towards an aesthetics of transmediality', in W. Buckland (ed.) *Film Theory Goes to the Movies 2*. London: Routledge, 86–102.

Bruno, G. (1991) 'Heresies: The Body of Pasolini's Semiotics', in *Cinema Journal*, 30, 3, 29–42.

___ (2002) *Atlas of Emotion: Journeys in Art, Architecture, and Film*. London: Verso.

Buchanan, I. and P. MacCormack (eds) (2008) *Deleuze and the Schizo-*

analysis of Cinema. London: Continuum.

Buckland, W. (2000a) *Film Theory and Contemporary Hollywood Movies*. New York and London: Routledge.

___ (2000b) *The Cognitive Semiotics of Film*. Cambridge: Cambridge University Press.

____ (2004) 'Film Semiotics', in R. Stam and T. Miller (eds) (2004) *A Companion to Film Theory*. Malden: Blackwell, 84–104.

___ (2012a) *Film Theory: Rational Reconstructions*. New York: Routledge.

___ (2012b) 'Solipsistic Film Criticism. Review of The Language and Style of Film Criticism', in *New Review of Film and Television Studies*, 10, 288–98 [Online: http://www.tandfonline.com/doi/full/10.1080/1740 0309.2012.672128]

Bunyard, T. (2012) 'Technoreformism', in *Radical Philosophy*, 174 [Online: http://www.radicalphilosophy.com/web/technoreformism]

Burch, N. (1973 [1969]) *Theory of Film Practice*, trans. H. R. Lane. London: Secker & Warburg.

Butler, A. (2002) *Women's Cinema: The Contested Screen*. London and New York: Wallflower Press.

Butler, J. (1993) *Bodies that Matter: On the Discursive Limits of Sex*. New York and London: Routledge.

Carrière, J.-C. (1994) *The Secret Language of Film*. New York: Pantheon.

Carroll, N. (1988a) 'Film/Mind Analogies: The Case of Hugo Munsterberg', in *Journal of Aesthetics and Art Criticism*, 46, 4, 489–99.

___ (1988b) *Mystifying Movies: Fads and Fallacies in Contemporary Film Theory*. New York: Columbia University Press.

___ (1996) *Theorizing the Moving Image*. Cambridge: Cambridge University Press.

Cartwright, L. (2008) *Moral Spectatorship: Technologies of Voice and Affect in Postwar Representations of the Child*. Durham, NC: Duke University Press.

Casetti, F. (1999 [1993]) *Theories of Cinema 1945–1999*, trans. F. Chiotri, E. Gard Bartolini-Salimbeni with T. Kelso. Austin, TX: University of Texas Press.

Caslin, S. (2007) 'Compliance Fiction: Adorno and Horkheimer's "Culture Industry" Thesis in a Multimedia Age', in *Fast Capitalism*, 2, 2 [Online: http://www.uta.edu/huma/agger/fastcapitalism/2_2/caslin.html]

Chanan, M. (1983) *Twenty-Five Years of New Latin American Cinema*.

London: British Film Institute.

Chare, N. and L. Watkins (2012) 'The Matter of Film: Decasia and Lyrical Nitrate', in E. Barrett and B. Bolt (eds) *Carnal Knowledge: Towards a 'New Materialism'*. London: IB Tauris, 75–88.

Chaudhuri, S. (2005) *Contemporary World Cinema: Europe, the Middle East, East Asia and South Asia*. Edinburgh: Edinburgh University Press.

___ (2006) *Feminist Film Theorists: Laura Mulvey, Kaja Silverman, Teresa de Lauretis, Barbara Creed*. London: Routledge

Chaudhary, Z. R. (2009) 'Humanity Adrift: Race, Materiality, and Allegory in Alfonso Cuarón's *Children of Men*', in *Camera Obscura*, 24, 3, 72–109.

Chateau, D. (ed.) (2011) *Subjectivity: Filmic Representation and the Spectator's Experience*. Amsterdam: Amsterdam University Press.

Cherchi Usai, P. (2000) *Silent Cinema: An Introduction*. London: British Film Institute.

___ (2001) *The Death of Cinema: History, Cultural Memory and the Digital Dark Age*. London: British Film Institute.

___ (2007) '*Passio*: An Interview with Paolo Cherchi Usai by Grant McDonald', in Rouge (10). [Online: http://www.rouge.com.au/10/passio.html]

Cheuk, P. T. (2008) *Hong Kong New Wave Cinema (1978–2000)*. Bristol: Intellect.

Chen, Y-H. (2009) 'Michael Haneke's Cinema: The Ethic of the Image by Catherine Wheatley', in *Senses of Cinema*, 53, December [Online: http://sensesofcinema.com/2009/book-reviews/michael-hanekes-cinema-the-ethic-of-the-image-by-catherine-wheatley/]

Chion, M. (2005 [1994]) *Audio-Vision: Sound on Screen*, trans. C. Gorbman. New York: Columbia University Press.

___ (2009) *Film: A Sound Art*, trans. C. Gorbman and C. J. Delogou. New York: Columbia University Press.

Choi, J. and M. Frey (2013) *Cine-Ethics: Ethical Dimensions of Film Theory, Practice, and Spectatorship*. London: Routledge.

Clayton, A. and A. Klevan (2012) 'Authors' Reply to Warren Buckland, "Solipsistic film criticism"' [Online: http://bristol.academia.edu/AlexClayton/Papers/1946470/Authors_Reply_to_Warren_Bucklands_Review_of_The_Language_and_Style_of_Film_Criticism]

Codell, J. F. (ed.) (2006) *Genre, Gender, Race and World Cinema*. Oxford: Blackwell.

Colebrook, C. (2014) *Death of the PostHuman: Essays on Extinction, Vol. 1*. Open Humanities Press [Online: http://openhumanitiespress.org/essays-on-extinction-vol1.html]

Collins, F. and T. Davis (2004) *Australian Cinema After Mabo*. Cambridge: Cambridge University Press.

Colman, F. (2009a) 'Introduction', in F. Colman (ed.) *Film, Theory and Philosophy*. Durham: Acumen, 1–15.

___ (2009b) 'The Western: Affective Sound Communities', in G. Harper, R. Doughty and J. Eisentraut (eds) *Sound and Music in Film and Visual Media*. New York and London: Continuum, 194–207.

___ (2011) *Deleuze and Cinema*. Oxford: Berg.

Connoly, M. (2009) *The Place of Artists' Cinema: Space, Site and Screen*. Bristol: Intellect.

Coole, D. and S. Frost (eds) (2010) *New Materialisms: Ontology, Agency, and Politics*. Durham, NC: Duke University Press.

Cooper, S. (2013) *The Soul of Film Theory*. Basingstoke: Palgrave Macmillan.

Cornwell, R. (1972) 'Some Formalist Tendencies in the Current American Avant-garde Film', in *Studio International*, 184, 948, 110–14.

Cowan, P. (2012) 'Authorship and the Director of Photography: A Case Study of Gregg Toland and Citizen Kane', in *Networking Knowledge*, 5, 1, 231–45.

Cox, D. and M. P. Levine (2002) *Thinking Through Film: Doing Philosophy, Watching Movies*. Chichester: Wiley-Blackwell.

Crary, J. (1990) *Techniques of the Observer: On Vision and Modernity in the Nineteenth Century*. Cambridge, MA: MIT Press.

Crawford, D. L. (2009) *A Windfall of Musicians: Hitler's Exiles and Emigres in Southern California*. New Haven, CT: Yale University Press.

Creed, B. (1993) *The Monstrous-Feminine: Film, Feminism, Psychoanalysis*. London: Routledge.

___ (1996 [1986]) 'Horror and the Monstrous-Feminine: An Imaginary Abjection', in B. K. Grant (ed.) *The Dread of Difference: Gender and the Horror Film*. Austin, TX: University of Texas Press, 35–65.

Crogan, P. (2010) 'Knowledge, care and trans-individuation: An interview with Bernard Stiegler', in *Cultural Politics: An International Journal*, 6, 2, 157–70.

Cua Lim, B. (2009) *Translating Time: Cinema, the Fantastic and Temporal*

Critique. Durham, NC: Duke University Press.

Cubitt, S. (2004) *The Cinema Effect*. Cambridge, MA: MIT Press.

Curtis, D. (2007) *A History of Artists Film & Video in Britain*. London: British Film Institute.

Dash, J. (1992) 'Making Daughters of the Dust', *Daughters of the Dust. The Making of An African American Woman's Film*. New York: The New Press, 1–26.

Debord, G. (1994 [1967]) *The Society of the Spectacle*, trans. Donald Nicholson-Smith. New York: Zone.

De Brigard, E. (1975) 'The History of Ethnographic Film', in P. Hockings (ed.) *Principles of Visual Anthropology*. The Hague: Mouton, 13–43.

De Bruyn, D. (2012) 'Recovering the Hidden Through Found-Footage Films', in E. Barrett and B. Bolt (eds) *Carnal Knowledge: Towards a 'New Materialism'*. London: IB Tauris, 89–101.

De Lauretis, T. (1984) *Alice Doesn't: Feminism, Semiotics, Cinema*. Bloomington, IN: Indiana University Press.

___ (1986 [1978]) 'Through the Looking-Glass', in P. Rosen (ed.) *Narrative, Apparatus, Ideology*. New York: Columbia University Press, 360–72.

___ (1987) *Technologies of Gender: Essays on Theory, Film, and Fiction*. Bloomington, IN: Indiana University Press.

___ (1995) 'On the Subject of Fantasy', in L. Pietropaolo and A. Testaferri (eds) *Feminisms in the Cinema*. Bloomington, IN: Indiana University Press, 63–85.

___ (2004) 'Statement Due', in *Critical Inquiry*, 30, 2, 365–8 [Online: http://www.jstor.org/stable/10.1086/421134]

De Lauretis, T. and S. Heath (eds) (1980) *The Cinematographic Apparatus*. New York: St. Martin's Press.

Deleuze, G. (1986 [1983]) *Cinema 1: The Movement-Image*, trans. H. Tomlinson and B. Habberjam. London: Athlone.

___ (1989 [1985]) *Cinema 2: The Time-Image*, trans. H. Tomlinson and R. Galeta. London: Athlone.

Deleuze, G. and F. Guattari (1987 [1980]) *A Thousand Plateaus*, trans. B. Massumi. Minneapolis, MS: University of Minnesota Press.

Deledalle, G. (2000) *Charles S. Peirce's Philosophy of Signs: Essays in Comparative Semiotics*. Bloomington, IN: Indiana University Press.

Derrida, J. (1976 [1967]) *Of Grammatology*, trans. G. Spivak. Baltimore, MD: Johns Hopkins University Press.

___ (1978 [1967]) *Writing and Difference*, trans. A. Bass. Chicago: University of Chicago Press.

Desser, D. (1988) *Eros Plus Massacre: Introduction to Japanese New Wave Cinema*. Bloomington, IN: Indiana University Press.

Diawara, M. (1993 [1988]) 'Black Spectatorship: Problems of Identification and Resistance', in M. Diawara (ed.) *Black American Cinema*. New York: Routledge, 211–20.

Doane, M. A. (1985 [1980]) 'The Voice in Cinema: The Articulation of Body and Space', in E. Wies and J. Belton (eds) *Film Sound: Theory and Practice*. New York: Columbia University Press, 162–76.

___ (1987) *The Desire to Desire: The Women's Film of the 1940s*. Basingstoke: Macmillan.

___ (2002) *The Emergence of Cinematic Time: Modernity, Contingency, the Archive*. Cambridge, MA: Harvard University Press.

Doane, M. A. and J. Bergstrom (eds) (1989) 'The Spectatrix', special issue of *Camera Obscura*, 20/21.

Downing, J. D. H. (1986) *Film and Politics in the Third World*. New York: Autonomedia.

Downing, L. and L. Saxton (2009) *Film and Ethics: Foreclosed Encounters*. London: Routledge.

Drummond, P., A. L. Rees, B. Hein, W. Herzogenrath, M. Le Grice, I. Christie, P. Weibel, D. Dusinberre and W. Moritz (1979) *Film as Film: Formal Experiment in Film, 1910–1975*. Exhibition Catalogue (3 May–17 June). London: Hayward Gallery.

Dulac, Germaine (1978 [1925]) 'The Essence of the Cinema: The Visual Idea', trans. R. Lamberton, in P. A. Sitney (ed.) *The Avant-Garde Film: A Reader of Theory and Criticism*. New York: New York University Press, 36–42.

Duong, L. P. (2012) *Treacherous Subjects: Gender, Culture, and Trans-Vietnamese Feminism*. Philadelphia, PA: Temple University Press.

Dusek, V. (2006) *Philosophy of Technology*. Malden: Blackwell.

Dyer, R. (2001) *The Culture of Queers*. London and New York: Routledge.

___ (2002 [1992]) 'Entertainment and Utopia', in S.Cohan (ed.) *Hollywood Musicals: The Film Reader*. London and New York: Routledge, 19–30.

Dzialo, C. (2009) '"Frustrated Time" Narration: The Screenplays of Charlie Kaufman', in W. Buckland (ed.) *Puzzle Films: Complex Storytelling in Contemporary Cinema*. Chichester: Wiley-Blackwell, 107–28.

Ehrat, J. (2004) *Cinema and Semiotic: Peirce and Film Aesthetics, Narration and Representation*. Toronto: University of Toronto Press.

Eisenstein, S. (1977 [1949]) *Film Form: Essays in Film Theory*, trans. and ed. J. Leyda. New York: Harcourt.

Elcott, N. M. (2011) 'On Cinematic Invisibility: Expanded Cinema Between Wagner and Television', in A. L. Rees, D. White, S. Ball and D. Curtis (eds) *Expanded Cinema: Art, Performance, Film*. London: Tate, 39–49.

Eleftheriotis, D. (2010) *Cinematic Journeys: Film and Movement*. Edinburgh: Edinburgh University Press.

Ellul, J. (1967 [1954]) *The Technological Society. La Technique: L'enjeu du siècle*, trans. J. Wilkinson. London: Vintage Books.

Elsaesser, T. (1989) *New German Cinema: A History*. New Brunswick, NJ: Rutgers University Press.

___ (2004) 'The New Film History as Media Archaeology', in *Cinémas: revue d'études cinématographiques/Cinémas: Journal of Film Studies*, 14, 2/3, 75–117 [Online: http://isites.harvard.edu/fs/docs/icb.topic 591072.files/Elsaesser%20II.pdf]

___ (2009) 'The Mind-Game Film', in W. Buckland (ed.) *Puzzle Films: Complex Storytelling in Contemporary* Cinema. Oxford: Wiley-Blackwell: 13–41.

___ (2013) *German Cinema – Terror and Trauma: Cultural Memory Since 1945*. New York: Routledge.

Elsaesser, T. and A. Barker (1990) *Early Cinema: Space, Frame, Narrative*. London: British Film Institute.

Elsaesser, T. and M. Hagener (2010) *Film Theory: An Introduction Through the Senses*. New York: Routledge.

Etherington-Wright, C. and R. Doughty (2011) *Understanding Film Theory*. Basingstoke: Palgrave Macmillan.

Feenberg, A. (1999) *Questioning Technology*. London and New York: Routledge.

Fischer, L. (1989) *Shot/Countershot: Film Tradition and Women's Cinema*. Princeton, NJ: Princeton University Press.

Fossati, G. (2014) *From Grain to Pixel: The Archival Life of Film in Transition* (second edition). Amsterdam: Amsterdam University Press.

Foucault, M. (1978 [1976]) *The History of Sexuality. Volume I: An Introduction*, trans. R. Hurley. London: Penguin.

___ (2008) (Lectures at the College de France), ed. M. Senellart, trans. G.

Burchell. Basingstoke: Palgrave Macmillan.

Frampton, D. (2006) *Filmosophy*. London and New York: Wallflower Press.

Frey, M. (2003) 'Michael Haneke', in *Senses of Cinema*, 'Great Directors 28', October [Online: http://sensesofcinema.com/2003/great-directors/haneke-2/]

Friedberg, A. (1993) *Window Shopping: Cinema and the Postmodern*. Berkeley, CA: University of California Press.

___ (2006) *The Virtual Window: From Alberti to Microsoft*. Cambridge, MA: MIT Press.

Furstenau, M. (2010) 'Introduction Film Theory: A History of Debates', in M. Furstenau (ed.) *The Film Theory Reader: History and Debates*. London and New York: Routledge, 1–20.

Gabriel, T. (1982) *Third Cinema in the Third World*. Ann Arbor: UMI Press.

Galt, R. (2006) *The New European Cinema: Redrawing the Map*. New York: Columbia University Press.

Gaston, S. and I. Maclachlan (eds) (2011) *Reading Derrida's Of Grammatology*. London and New York: Continuum.

Gee, J. P. (2010) *An Introduction to Discourse Analysis: Theory and Method*. (third edition). London: Routledge.

Geller, C. (2005) 'Grizzly Man' [Review], in *Cineaste*, Winter, 52–3.

Genosko, G. (2009) 'Félix Guattari', in F. Colman (ed.) *Film, Theory and Philosophy*. Durham: Acumen, 243–52.

Gidal, P. (1976) 'Theory and Definition of Structural/Materialist Film', in *Structural Film Anthology*. London: British Film Institute [Online: http://www.luxonline.org.uk/articles/theory_and_definition(1).html]

___ (1989) *Materialist Film*. London and New York: Routledge.

Gledhill, C. (1988) 'Pleasurable Negotiations', in E. D. Pribram (ed.) *Female Spectators: Looking at Film and Television*. London: Verso: 64–89.

Gledhill, C. and L. Williams (eds) (2000) *Reinventing Film Studies*. London: Arnold.

Gomery, D. (1992) *Shared Pleasures: A History of Movie Presentation in the United States*. Madison, WS: University of Wisconsin Press.

Grau, O. and T. Veigl (2011) *Imagery in the 21st Century*. Cambridge, MA: MIT Press.

Grønstad, A. (2002) 'The Appropriational Fallacy: Grand Theories and the Neglect of Film Form', in *Film Philosophy*, 6, 23 [Online: http://www.film-philosophy.com/vol6-2002/n23gronstad]

___ (2011) *Screening the Unwatchable: Spaces of Negation in Post-Millennial Art Cinema*. Basingstoke: Palgrave Macmillan.

Guardian, The (2003) 'Message in a Movie', 7 April [Online: http://www.theguardian.com/film/2003/apr/07/artsfeatures.immigrationand publicservices]

Guattari, F. (1995 [1992]) *Chaosmosis*, trans. P. Bains and J. Pefanis. Bloomington, IN: Indiana University Press.

___ (2008) *Chaosophy: Texts and Interviews 1972–1977*. Cambridge, MA: MIT Press.

___ (2013 [1989]) *Schizoanalytic Cartographies*, trans. A. Goffey. London: Continuum.

Guneratne, A. R. and W. Dissanayake (eds) (2003) *Rethinking Third Cinema*. New York: Routledge.

Gunning, T. (1986) 'The Cinema of Attractions: Early Film, Its Spectator and the Avant-Garde', in *Wide Angle*, 8, 3/4, 63–70.

Halberstam, J. (2011) *The Queer Art of Failure*. Durham, NC: Duke University Press.

Hall, S. (1989) 'Cultural Identity and Cinematic Representation' in R. Stam and T. Miller (eds) *Film and Theory: An Anthology*. Malden, MA: Blackwell, 704–14.

Hansen, M. (2004) '"Realtime Synthesis" and the Différance of the Body: Technocultural Studies in the Wake of Deconstruction', in *Culture Machine*, 6 [Online: http://www.culturemachine.net/index.php/cm/article/viewArticle/9/8]

Hansen, M. B. (1991) *Babel and Babylon: Spectatorship in American Silent Film*. Cambridge, MA: University of Harvard Press.

___ (1993) '"With Skin and Hair": Kracauer's Theory of Film, Marseille 1940', in *Critical Inquiry*, 19, 3, 437–69 [Online: http://www.jstor.org/stable/1343960]

___ (2012) *Cinema and Experience: Siegfried Kracauer, Walter Benjamin, and Theodor W. Adorno*. Berkeley, CA: University of California Press.

Haraway, D. J. (1991 [1984]) *Simians, Cyborgs, and Women: The Reinvention of Nature*. London: Free Association Books.

Harbord, J. (2007) *The Evolution of Film: Rethinking Film Studies*. London: Polity Press.

Harper, G., R. Doughty, J. Eisentraut (eds) (2006) *Sound and Music in Film and Visual Media*. New York and London: Continuum.

Hayles, K. N. (1999) *How We Became Posthuman: Virtual Bodies in Cyber-netics, Literature, and Informatics*. Chicago: University of Chicago Press.

___ (2005) *My Mother was a Computer: Digital Subjects and Literary Texts*. Chicago, IL: University of Chicago Press.

Hayward, S. (2000) *Cinema Studies: The Key Concepts* (second edition). London and New York: Routledge.

Heath, S. (1981) *Questions of Cinema*. Bloomington, IN: Indiana University Press.

Heath, S. and P. Mellencamp (eds) (1983) *Cinema and Language*. Milwaukee, WS: University of Wisconsin Press.

Heller-Nicholas, A. (2011) *Rape-Revenge Films: A Critical Study*. Jefferson, NC: McFarland.

Hines, C. and D. Kerr (2012) *Hard to Swallow: Hard-core Pornography on Screen*. London and New York: Wallflower Press.

Hjort, M. and S. MacKenzie (2003) *Purity and Provocation: Dogma 95*. London: British Film Institute.

Hongisto, I. (2012) 'Moments of Affection: Jayce Salloum's *everything and nothing* and the Thresholds of Testimonial Video', in E. Barrett and B. Bolt (eds) *Carnal Knowledge: Towards a 'New Materialism'*. London: IB Tauris, 105–12.

hooks, b. (1990) *Yearning: race, gender, and cultural politics*. Toronto: Between the Lines.

___ (1992) *Black Looks: Race and Representation*. London: Turnaround.

___ (1996) 'The oppositional gaze: black female spectators', in b. hooks, *Reel to Reel: Race, Sex, and Class at the Movies*. London and New York: Routledge, 197–213.

Holt, N. (2011 [1975]) 'Pine Barrens', in *Nancy Holt: Sightlines.*, ed. A. J. Williams. Berkeley, CA: University of California Press, 248–51.

Hubbs, N. (2004) *The Queer Composition of America's Sound: Gay Modernists, American Music, and National Identity*. Berkeley, CA: University of California Press.

Humm, M. (1997) *Feminism and Film*. Bloomington, IN: Indiana University Press.

Ito, M., D. Okabe and I. Tsuji (eds) (2012) *Fandom Unbound: Otaku Culture in a Connected World*. New Haven, CT: Yale University Press.

Jay, M. (1994) *Downcast Eyes: The Denigration of Vision in Twentieth-*

Century French Thought. Berkeley, CA: University of California Press.

Jenkins, B. (1978) 'What Price Normalization?' [review of *The Major Film Theories*] in *Jump Cut*, 18 [Online: http://www.ejumpcut.org/archive/onlinessays/JC18folder/DudleyAndrew.html]

Jenkins, H. (2006) *Convergence Culture: Where Old and New Media Collide.* New York: New York University Press.

Jin, D. Y. (2006) 'Cultural politics in Korea's contemporary films under neoliberal globalization', in *Media, Culture & Society*, 28, 1, 5–23.

Johnston, C. (1976 [1973]) 'Women's Cinema as Counter-Cinema', in B. Nichols (ed.) *Movies and Methods*. Berkeley, CA: University of California Press, 208–17.

Kael, P. (1966) *I Lost It at the Movies.* London: Cape.

Kaplan, E. A. (1983) *Women and Film: Both Sides of the Camera.* New York: Methuen.

___ (1990) *Psychoanalysis and Cinema.* New York: Routledge.

___ (1997) *Looking for the Other: Feminism, Film and the Imperial Gaze.* New York: Routledge.

Kaplan, E. A. and B. Wang (2010) *Trauma and Cinema: Cross-Cultural Explorations.* Hong Kong: Hong Kong University Press.

Keeling, K. (2007) *The Witch's Flight: The Cinematic, the Black Femme, and the Image of Common Sense.* Durham, NC: Duke University Press.

Kellner, D. (1999) 'Virilio, War and Technology: Some Critical Reflections', in *Theory, Culture & Society*, 16, 5/6, 103–25.

Kember, S. (2011) 'No Humans Allowed? The alien in/as feminist theory', in *Feminist Theory*, 12, 183–201.

Kember, S. and J. Zylinska (2012) *Life After New Media: Mediation as a Vital Process.* Cambridge, MA: MIT Press.

Klevan, A. (2000) *Disclosure of the Everyday: Undramatic Achievement in Narrative Film.* Trowbridge: Flicks Books.

Kracauer, S. (1997 [1960]) *Theory of Film: The Redemption of Physical Reality.* London: Oxford University Press.

___ (1999 [1960]) 'The Establishment of Physical Existence', in L. Braudy and M. Cohen (eds) *Film Theory and Criticism: Introductory Readings.* New York and Oxford: Oxford University Press, 292–303.

Kristeva, J. (1982 [1980]) *The Powers of Horror: An Essay on Abjection.* New York: Columbia University Press.

___ (1986) *The Kristeva Reader*, ed. T. Moi. New York: Columbia University

Press.

Krocker, A. (2012) *Body Drift: Butler, Hayles, Haraway*. Minneapolis, MS: University of Minnesota Press.

Kuhn, A. (1982) *Women's Pictures: Feminism and the Cinema*. London: Routledge and Kegan Paul.

Kuhn, A. and K. McAllister (eds) (2006) *Locating Memory: Photographic Acts*. Oxford: Berghahn.

Kuhn, A. and A. Wolpe (eds) (1978) *Feminism and Materialism: Women and Modes of Production*. London: Routledge and Kegan Paul.

Lamarre, T. (2009) *The Anime Machine: A Media Theory of Animation*. Minneapolis, MS: University of Minnesota Press.

Lapsley, R. and M. Westlake (2006) *Film Theory: An Introduction* (second edition). Manchester: Manchester University Press.

Lebedeva, K. (2009) 'Review: Bernard Stiegler, *Technics and Time, 2: Disorientation*', in *Parrhesia*, 7, 81–5.

Lechte, J. (2012) *Genealogy and Ontology of the Western Image and its Digital Future*. New York: Routledge.

Le Grice, M. (2001) *Experimental Cinema in the Digital Age*. London: British Film Institute.

Leibman, S. (1981) *Paul Sharits*. St. Paul: Walker Art Center.

Leotta, A. (2011) *Touring the Screen: Tourism and New Zealand Film Geographies*. Bristol: Intellect.

Linville, S. E. (1998 [1991]) 'Retrieving History: Margarethe Von Trotta's *Marianne and Juliane*', in *Feminism, Film, Fascism*. Austin, TX: University of Texas Press, 84–108.

Lyon, E. (1988) 'The Cinema of Lol V. Stein', in C. Penley (ed.) *Feminism and Film Theory*. London: Routledge, 244–73.

Lyotard (1986 [1973]) 'Acinema', trans. P. N. Livingston, in P. Rosen (ed.) *Narrative, Apparatus, Ideology*. New York: Columbia University Press, 349–59.

MacCormack, P. (2008) *Cinesexuality*. London: Ashgate.

___ (2012) *Posthuman Ethics*. London: Ashgate.

Madrigal, A. C. (2014) 'How Netflix Reverse Engineered Hollywood', in *The Atlantic* [Online: http://m.theatlantic.com/technology/archive/2014/01/how-netflix-reverse-engineered-hollywood/282679/]

Malabou, C. (2010) *Plasticity at the Dusk of Writing: Dialectic, Destruction, Deconstruction*. New York: Columbia University Press.

Manovich, L. (2001) *The Language of New Media*. Cambridge, MA: MIT Press.

___ (2012) 'What is Digital Cinema?' [Online: http://www.manovich.net/ TEXT/digital-cinema.html]

Marciniak, K., A. Imre and A. O'Healy (eds) (2007) *Transnational Feminism in Film and Media*. Basingstoke: Palgrave Macmillan.

Margulies, I. (1996) *Nothing Happens: Chantal Akerman's Hyperrealist Everyday*. Durham, NC: Duke University Press.

Marks, L. U. (1998) 'Video haptics and erotics', in *Screen*, 39, 331–48.

Martin, S. (2011) *New Waves in Cinema*. Harpenden: Kamera Books.

Martin-Jones, D. (2011) *Deleuze and World Cinemas*. London and New York: Continuum.

Mazumdar, R. (2012) 'Film stardom after liveness', in *Continuum: Journal of Media & Cultural Studies*, 26, 6, 833–44 [Online: http:/ / dx.doi.org/ 10.1080/ 10304312.2012.731258]

McCabe, J. (2004) *Feminist Film Studies: Writing the Woman into Cinema*. London and New York: Wallflower Press.

McGlotten, S. and S. Vangundy (2013) 'Zombie Porn 1.0: Or, Some Queer Things Zombie Sex Can Teach Us', in *Qui Parle: Critical Humanities and Social Sciences*, 21, 2, 101–25 [Online: http://www.jstor.org/ stable/10.5250/quiparle.21.2.0101]

Mekas, (1971 [1959]) 'A Call for a New Generation of Film-Makers', in P. A. Sitney (ed.) *Film Culture: An Anthology*. London: Secker & Warburg, 73–5.

Mellencamp, P. (1990) *Indiscretions: Avant-Garde Film, Video, and Feminism*. Bloomington, IN: Indiana University Press.

___ (1993/94) 'Haunted History: Tracey Moffatt and Julie Dash', in *Discourse: Theoretical Studies in Media and Culture*, 16, 2, 127–63.

Merck, M. (ed.) (1992) *The Sexual Subject: A Screen Reader in Sexuality*. London: Routledge.

Metz, C. (1974a) *Film Language: A Semiotics of the Cinema*, trans. M. Taylor. New York: Oxford University Press.

___ (1974b) *Language and Cinema*, trans. D. J. Umiker-Sebeok. The Hague: Mouton.

___ (1979) 'The Cinematic Apparatus as a Social Institution: An Interview with Christian Metz', in *Discourse: Journal for Theoretical Studies in Media and Culture*, 3, 7–38.

___ (1982 [1975]) *The Imaginary Signifier: Psychoanalysis and the Cinema.* Bloomington, IN: Indiana University Press.

___ (1991) *Film Language.* Chicago: University of Chicago Press.

Michelson, A. (ed.) (1971) *Artforum*, 'Special Film Issue', September.

Minh-Ha, T. (1991) *When the Moon Waxes Red: Representation, Gender, and Cultural Politics.* London: Routledge.

Modleski, T. (2005 [1988]) *The Women Who Knew Too Much: Hitchcock and Feminist Theory* (second edition). London and New York: Routledge.

Mroz, M. (2013) *Temporality and Film Analysis.* Edinburgh: Edinburgh University Press.

Mullarkey, J. (2009) *Refractions of Reality: Philosophy and the Moving Image.* Basingstoke: Palgrave Macmillan.

Mulvey, L. (1986 [1975]) 'Visual Pleasure and Narrative Cinema', in P. Rosen (ed.) *Narrative, Apparatus, Ideology.* New York: Columbia University Press, 198–209.

___ (1988 [1981]) 'Afterthoughts on "Visual Pleasure and Narrative Cinema" inspired by *Duel in the Sun*', in C. Penley (ed.) *Feminism and Film Theory.* New York: Routledge/British Film Institute, 69–79.

Munsterberg, H. (1970) *The Film: A Psychological Study.* New York: Dover Publications.

Murch, W. (2001) *In the Blink of an Eye: A Perspective on Film Editing.* Los Angeles: Silman-James Press.

Naficy, H. (2001) *An Accented Cinema: Exilic and Diasporic Filmmaking.* Princeton, NJ: Princeton University Press.

Nagib, L. (2006) 'Towards a Positive Definition of World Cinema', in S. Dennison and S. H. Lim (eds) *Remapping World Cinema: Identity, Culture and Politics in Film.* London and New York: Wallflower Press, 30–7.

Nerenberg, E. (2006) *Murder Made in Italy: Homicide, Media, and Contemporary Italian Culture.* Bloomington, IN: Indiana University Press.

Ndalianis, A. (2006) 'Tomorrow's World That We Shall Build Today', in R. Pepperell and M. Punt (eds) *Screen Consciousness: Cinema, Mind and World.* Amsterdam and New York: Rodopi, 41–64.

Nichols, B. (1991) *Representing Reality: Issues and Concepts in Documentary.* Bloomington, IN: Indiana University Press.

___ (2001) *Introducing the Documentary.* Bloomington, IN: Indiana

University Press.

Nieland, J. (2001) 'Graphic Violence: Native Americans and the Western Archive in Dead Man', in *The New Centennial Review*, 1, 2, 171–200.

Noys, B. (2007) 'Antiphusis: Werner Herzog's *Grizzly Man*', in *Film-Philosophy* (11.3 November) [Online: http://www.film-philosophy.com/2007v11n3/noys.pdf]

O'Pray, M. (2003) *Avant-Garde Film: Forms, Themes and Passions*. London and New York: Wallflower Press.

Orr, J. (2009) 'Michael Haneke's Cinema: The Ethic of the Image', in *Screen*, 50, 468–71.

Pandian, A. (2013) 'In the Light of Experience: An Indian Cameraman', in *BioScope: South Asian Screen Studies*, 4, 1, 81–92.

Parks, L. (2005) *Cultures in Orbit: Satellites and the Televisual*. Durham, NC: Duke University Press.

Parikka, J. and G. Hertz (2010) 'Resetting Theory: CTheory Interview', in *Ctheory* [Online: www.ctheory.net/articles.aspx?id=631]

Pasolini, P. P. (2005 [1972]) *Heretical Empiricism*, trans. B. Lawton and L. K. Barnett. Washington, DC: New Academia Press.

Penley, C. (1975a) 'Film Language by Christian Metz: Semiology's Radical Possibilities', in *Jump Cut*, 5, 18–19 [Online: http://www.ejumpcut.org/archive/onlinessays/JC05folder/FilmLangMetz.html]

Penley, C. (1975b) (ed.) *Feminism and Film Theory*. New York: Routledge/British Film Institute.

Petric, V. (1993) *Constructivism in Film – A Cinematic Analysis: The Man with the Movie Camera*. Cambridge: Cambridge University Press.

Pick, A. (2011) *Creaturely Poetics: Animality and Vulnerability in Literature and Film*. New York: Columbia University Press.

Pick, A. and G. Narraway (eds) (2013) *Screening Nature: Cinema Beyond the Human*. London: Berghahn.

Pisters, P. (2011) *The Neuro-Image: A Deleuzian Filmphilosophy of Digital Screen Culture*. Redwood City, CA: Stanford University Press.

Polan, D. (1987) 'Film Theory Re-Assessed', in *Continuum: The Australian Journal of Media & Culture*, 1, 2 [Online: http://wwwmcc.murdoch.edu.au/ReadingRoom/1.2/Polan.html]

___ (2007) *Scenes of Instruction: The Beginnings of the U.S. Study of Film*. Berkeley, CA: University of California Press.

Porton, R. (1999) *Film and the Anarchist Imagination*. New York: Verso.

Projansky, S. (2001) *Watching Rape: Film and Television in Postfeminist Culture*. New York: New York University Press.

Rancière, J. (2004) *The Politics of Aesthetics: The Distribution of the Sensible*, trans. G. Rockhill. London and New York: Continuum.

___ (2006) *Film Fables*. trans. E. Battista. Oxford: Berg.

___ (2009 [2008]) *The Emancipated Spectator*, trans. G. Elliott. London: Verso.

Rascaroli, L., G. Young and B. Monahan (2014) *Amateur Filmmaking: The Home Movie, the Archive, the Web*. London: Bloomsbury.

Ravetto, K. (2001) *The Unmasking of Fascist Aesthetics*. Minneapolis, MN: University of Minnesota Press.

Renov, M. (2004) *The Subject of Documentary*. Minneapolis, MS: University of Minnesota Press.

Rich, B. R. (1998) *Chick Flicks: Theories and Memories of a Feminist Film Movement*. Durham, NC: Duke University Press.

___ (2005b) *New Punk Cinema*. Edinburgh: Edinburgh University Press.

Roberts, B. (2006) 'Cinema as mnemotechnics: Bernard Stiegler and the industrialization of memory', in *Angelaki*, 11, 1, 55–63.

___ (2012) 'Technics, Individuation and Tertiary Memory: Bernard Stiegler's Challenge to Media Theory', in *New Formations*, 77, 8–20.

Rodowick, D. N. (1991) *The Difficulty of Difference: Psychoanalysis, Sexual Difference and Film Theory*. New York: Routledge.

___ (1994) *The Crisis of Political Modernism: Criticism and Ideology in Contemporary Film Theory*. Berkeley, CA: University of California Press.

___ (2007) *The Virtual Life of Film*. Cambridge, MA: Harvard University Press.

___ (2010) 'An Elegy for Theory', in M. Furstenau (ed.) *The Film Theory Reader: History and Debates*. London and New York: Routledge, 23–37.

___ (2013) 'The Value of Being Disagreeable', in *Critical Inquiry*, 39, 3, 592–613 [Online: http://www.jstor.org/stable/10.1086/670047]

___ (2014) *Elegy for Theory*. Cambridge, MA: Harvard University Press.

Rombes, N. (2005a) 'Avant-Garde Realism', in *CTheory*. [Online: www.ctheory.net/articles.aspx?id=442]

Rony, F. T. (1996) *The Third Eye: Race, Cinema, and Ethnographic Spectacle*. Durham, NC: Duke University Press.

Rosen, P. (ed.) (1986) *Narrative, Apparatus, Ideology.* New York: Columbia University Press.

Ruiz, R. (1995) *Poetics of Cinema*, trans. B. Holmes. Paris: DisVoir.

Rushton, R. (2009) 'Christian Metz', in F. Colman (ed.) *Film, Theory and Philosophy.* Durham: Acumen, 266–75.

___ (2011) *The Reality of Film: Theories of Filmic Reality.* Manchester: Manchester University Press.

Rushton, R. and G. Bettinson (2010) *What is Film Theory?* Maidenhead: McGraw-Hill/Open University Press.

Russell, C. (1999) *Experimental Ethnography: The Work of Film in the Age of Video.* Durham, NC: Duke University Press.

Rust, S., S. Monani and S. Cubitt (eds) (2012) *Ecocinema Theory and Practice.* London and New York: Routledge.

Salt, B. (2006) *Moving into Pictures: More on Film History, Style, and Analysis.* London: Starword.

___ (2009 [1983]) *Film Style and Technology: History and Analysis* (third edition). London: Starword.

Saxton, L. (2008) *Haunted Images: Film, Ethics, Testimony and the Holocaust.* London and New York: Wallflower Press.

Schaeffer, P. (2004) 'Acousmatics', in C. Cox and D. Warner (eds) *Audio Culture: Readings in Modern Music.* New York and London: Continuum: 76–81.

Scholz, T. (ed.) (2013) *Digital Labor: The Internet as Playground and Factory.* New York: Routledge.

Schwartz, V. R. (1995) 'Cinematic Spectatorship before the Apparatus: The Public Taste for Reality in *Fin-de Siècle* Paris', in L. Charney and V. R. Schwartz (eds) *Cinema and the Invention of Modern Life.* Berkeley, CA: University of California Press, 297–319.

Sharits, P. (1972) 'Words per Page', in *Afterimage*, 4, 26–42.

Shaviro, S. (2010) *Post Cinematic Affect.* Washington, DC: Zero Books.

Shaw, D. (2008) *Film and Philosophy: Taking Movies Seriously.* London and New York: Wallflower Press.

Shohat, E. and R. Stam (eds) (2003) *Multiculturalism, Postcoloniality and Transnational Media.* New Brunswick, NJ: Rutgers University Press.

Silverman, K. (1986 [1983]) 'Suture', in P. Rosen (ed.) *Narrative, Apparatus, Ideology.* New York: Columbia University Press, 219–35.

Sinnerbrink, R. (2010) 'Disenfranchising film on the analytic-cognitivist turn in film theory', in J. Reynolds, E. Mares, J. Williams and J. Chase (eds) *Postanalytic and Metacontinental: Crossing Philosophical Divides.* London: Continuum, 173–89.

___ (2011) *New Philosophies of Film: Thinking Images.* New York: Continuum.

Sitney, P. A. (1970) *Michael Snow: A Survey.* Art Gallery of Ontario.

___ (ed.) (1971) *Film Culture: An Anthology.* London: Secker & Warburg.

___ (1974) *Visionary Film: The American Avant-Garde.* New York: Oxford University Press.

Slane, A. (1997) 'Romancing the System: women, narrative film, and the sexuality of computers', in J. Terry and M. Calvert (eds) *Processed Lives: Gender and Technology in Everyday Life.* London and New York: Routledge, 71–9.

Smelik, A. (2001) *And the Mirror Cracked: Feminist Cinema and Film Theory.* Palgrave Macmillan.

___ (2009) 'Lara Croft, *Kill Bill*, and feminist film studies', in R. Buikema and I. Van der Tuin (eds) *Doing Gender in Media, Art and Culture.* London and New York: Routledge, 178–92.

Smith, A. (1998) *Agnès Varda.* Manchester: Manchester University Press.

Smith, M. (1985) 'Modernism and the Avant-Garde', in *Wide Angle*, 7, 1/2), 395–412.

___ (2010) 'Film Theory Meets Analytic Philosophy; or, Film Studies and l'affaire Sokal', in *Cinema: The Journal of Philosophy and the Moving Image*, 1, 111–17.

Sobchack, V. (2004) *Carnal Thoughts: Embodiment and Moving Image Culture.* Berkeley, CA: University of California Press.

Solanas, F. and O. Gettino (2000 [1969]) 'Towards a Third Cinema', in R. Stam and T. Miller (eds) *Film and Theory: An Anthology.* Malden, MA: Blackwell, 265–86.

Sontag, S. (2003) *Regarding the Pain of Others.* New York: Farrar, Straus and Giroux.

Speilmann, Y. (2008) *Video: The Reflexive Medium.* Cambridge, MA: MIT Press.

Spivak, G. C. (1993) 'Foundations and Cultural Studies', in H. J. Silverman (ed.) *Questioning Foundations: Truth/Subjectivity/Culture.* New York and London: Routledge, 153–75.

Stack, O. (1969) *Pasolini on Pasolini.* London: Thames and Hudson/British

Film Institute.

Straayer, C. (1995) 'The Hypothetical Lesbian Heroine in Narrative Feature Film', in C. Creekmur, K. Doty and A. Doty (eds) *Out in Culture: Gay, Lesbian and Queer Essays on Popular Culture*. Durham, NC: Duke University Press, 44–59.

Stacey, J. (1993) *Star Gazing: Hollywood Cinema and Female Spectatorship*. London and New York: Routledge.

Staiger, J. (2000) *Perverse Spectators: The Practices of Film Reception*. New York: New York University Press.

Stam, R. (2000) *Film Theory: An Introduction*. Malden: Blackwell.

Stam, R., R. Burgoyne and S. Flitterman-Lewis (eds) (1992) *New Vocabularies in Film Semiotics: Structuralism, Post-structuralism and Beyond*. London and New York: Routledge.

Stam, R. and T. Miller (eds) (2000) *Film and Theory: An Anthology*. Oxford: Wiley-Blackwell.

___ (eds) (2004) *A Companion to Film Theory*. Malden: Blackwell.

Stevenson, J. (2002) *Lars von Trier*. London: British Film Institute.

Stiegler, B. (1998 [1994]) *Technics and Time 1: The Fault of Epimetheus*, trans. R. Beardsworth and G. Collins. Redwood City, CA: Stanford University Press.

___ (2009 [1996]) *Technics and Time, 2: Disorientation*, trans. S. Barker. Redwood City, CA: Stanford University Press.

___ (2010 [2009]) *For a New Critique of Political Economy*, trans. D. Ross. Cambridge: Polity Press.

___ (2011 [2001]) *Technics and Time 3: Cinematic Time and the Question of Malaise*, trans. S. Barker. Redwood City, CA: Stanford University Press.

___ (2012) 'Die Aufklärung in the Age of Philosophical Engineering', in *Computational Culture*, 2 [Online: http://computationalculture.net/comment/die-aufklarung-in-the-age-of-philosophical-engineering]

Stiegler, B. and J. Derrida (2002) *Echographies of Television*, trans. J. Bajorek. London: Polity Press.

Stoller, P. (1992) *The Cinematic Griot: The Ethnography of Jean Rouch*. Chicago: University of Chicago Press.

Streible, D. (2013) 'Moving image history and the F-word; or, "digital film" is an oxymoron', in *Film History*, 25, 1, 227–35.

Thanouli, E. (2013) *Wag the Dog: A Study on Film and Reality in the Digital Age*. London: Bloomsbury.

Thornham, S. (2012) *What If I Had Been the Hero?: Investigating Women's Cinema*. London: British Film Institute.

Tong, J. (2001) 'Crisis of Ideology and the Disenchanted Eye: Pasolini and Bataille', in *Contretemps*, 2 May, 74–88.

Tormey, S. (2013) *Anti-capitalism: A Beginner's Guide*. London: Oneworld.

Van der Tuin, I. (2011) 'New feminist materialisms', in *Women's Studies International Forum*, 34, 4, 271–7 [Online: http://www.sciencedirect.com/science/article/pii/S0277539511000549]

Verrier, R. (2014) 'End of film: Paramount first studio to stop distributing film prints', in *Los Angeles Times* [Online: http://www.latimes.com/entertainment/envelope/cotown/la-et-ct-paramount-digital-20140117,0,493094,full.story#axzz2tZUxR1KK]

Vertov, D. (1985) *Kino-eye: The Writings of Dziga Vertov*, ed. A. Michelson, trans. K. O'Brien. Berkeley, CA: University of California Press.

Viano, M. (1993) *A Certain Realism: Making Use of Pasolini's Film Theory and Practice*. Berkeley, CA: University of California Press.

Virilio, P. (1989 [1984]) *War and Cinema: The Logistics of Perception*, trans. P. Camiller. London: Verso.

___ (2005 [1984]) *Negative Horizon: An Essay in Dromoscopy*, trans. M. Degener. London and New York: Continuum.

Walley, J. (2011) '"Not an Image of the Death of Film": Contemporary Expanded Cinema and Experimental Film', in A. L. Rees, D. White, S. Ball and D. Curtis (eds) *Expanded Cinema: Art, Performance, Film*. London: Tate, 241–51.

Walker, J. (2005) *Trauma Cinema: Documenting Incest and the Holocaust*. Berkeley, CA: University of California Press.

Watson, J. (2009) *Guattari's Diagrammatic Thought: Writing Between Lacan and Deleuze*. London and New York: Continuum.

Whannel, P. and P. Harcourt (eds) (1964) *Studies in the Teaching of Film Within Formal Education*. London: British Film Institute.

White, H. (1973) *Metahistory: The Historical Imagination in Nineteenth-Century Europe*. Baltimore, MD: Johns Hopkins University Press.

White, M. (2006) *The Body and the Screen: Theories of Internet Spectatorship*. Cambridge, MA: MIT.

Wheatley, C. (2009) *Michael Haneke's Cinema: The Ethic of the Image*. Oxford: Berghahn.

___ (2012) 'Domestic Invasion: Michael Haneke and Home Audiences', in

B. McCann and D. Sorfa (eds) *The Cinema of Michael Haneke: Europe Utopia*. London and New York: Wallflower Press, 10–23.

Williams, L. (1999) *Hard Core: Power, Pleasure, and the 'Frenzy of the Visible'* (expanded edition). Berkeley, CA: University of California Press.

___ (2008) *Screening Sex*. Durham, NC: Duke University Press.

Willis, H. (2005) *New Digital Cinema: Reinventing the Moving Image*. London and New York: Wallflower Press.

Wilson, G. M. (2013) *Seeing Fictions in Film: The Epistemology of Movies*. Oxford: Oxford University Press.

Winthrop-Young, G., I. Iurascu and J. Parikka (eds) (2013) *Theory, Culture & Society*, 'Special Issue: Cultural Techniques', 30, 6.

Wollen, P. (1969) *Signs and Meaning in the Cinema*. Bloomington, IN: Indiana University Press.

___ (1972) 'Godard and Counter-Cinema: Vent d'Est' in *Afterimage*, 7, 6–17.

___ (1976) '"Ontology" and "Materialism" in Film', in *Screen*, 17, 1, 7–25.

___ (2008 [1993]) *Raiding the Icebox: Reflections on Twentieth-Century Culture*. London: Verso.

Young, A. (2009) *The Scene of Violence: Cinema, Crime, Affect*. London: Routledge-Cavendish.

Young, L. (1995) *Fear of the Dark: 'Race', Gender and Sexuality in the Cinema*. New York and London: Routledge.

Zeng, H. (2012) *Semiotics of Exile in Contemporary Chinese Film*. Basingstoke: Palgrave Macmillan.

Zizek, S. (1992) *Enjoy Your Symptom! Jacques Lacan in Hollywood and Out*. New York and London: Routledge.

INDEX